Praise for *Bringing For*

Zoe Enser's *Bringing Forth the Bard* is an artful, accessible and fascinating guide to Shakespeare's work, drawing on the immense power and the utter joy of studying his writing in a properly academic way. Enser draws masterfully on the intertextuality of the Bard's work, weaving together excellent explanations and practical applications together with a range of superb case studies contributed by myriad subject experts. It is thoroughly expert, insightful and brimming with Enser's clear love of Shakespeare's work.

Bringing Forth the Bard is a resource I will return to time and time again, highlighter in hand, ready to share Enser's expert insights with my students. Bloom argues Shakespeare shapes the way we think about the world; this book shapes the way I think about Shakespeare. It is a triumph.

Amy Staniforth, Assistant Principal, Iceni Academy,
and co-author of *Ready to Teach: Macbeth*

Bringing Forth the Bard is a wonderful introduction to the joys and challenges of teaching young people about the work of England's most celebrated playwright. In this eminently readable book, Enser shares her vast knowledge of Shakespeare's creations and the ways in which teachers can make them accessible to young people. Whether you are teaching Shakespeare for the first time or searching for renewed inspiration, *Bringing Forth the Bard* will prove to be an insightful and invigorating read.

Christopher Such, author of *The Art and Science of Teaching Primary Reading*

Zoe Enser's *Bringing Forth the Bard* is erudite yet accessible, comprehensive yet pacey, and brimming with clever theory yet eminently practical. Essential for newer teachers, it features helpful insights and advice from expert teachers and will also offer enough new ideas to satisfy even the biggest Shakespeare aficionado. This book should go to the top of any English teacher's book wish list.

Mark Roberts, teacher of English, Carrickfergus Grammar School,
and author of *You Can't Revise for GCSE English!*

Bringing Forth the Bard is a welcome addition to the long line of books (in the tradition of Rex Gibson and James Stredder) about teaching Shakespeare in schools and colleges. Its pragmatic approach will appeal to teachers looking for practical material to use in the classroom. Many of the activities presented are entirely new and innovative. The book convinces us that Shakespeare is still relevant to young people in today's classrooms, and that study of his works can be part of the all-important inclusivity agenda. Busy teachers will welcome the useful summaries of contextual material, and students will enjoy the string of lively, contemporary cultural references employed by the author when discussing the plays. The book does not shy away from addressing necessary – if sometimes less popular – issues such as examination board requirements and 'cultural capital', but matters are always directed back to the most important concern of all: bringing Shakespeare's scripts to life in the classroom through creative activities which emphasise enjoyment of the plays' themes, linguistic techniques and dramatic methods.

Chris Green, Trustee and Director, British Shakespeare Association, and Chair of the BSA Education committee

Zoe Enser's *Bringing Forth the Bard* is a tour de force: an essential guide to help ensure that our students receive the best teaching when it comes to approaching Shakespeare. It is a text that allows its readers to consider, to analyse and to reflect on why Shakespeare is still relevant in our classrooms today. From discussing his context and influences as well as biblical and classical allusion to an exploration of symbols, motifs and stagecraft, Zoe deftly removes any barriers to understanding Shakespeare we may encounter, offering us a peek into parts of the Bard's world that are often ignored. This has clearly been a labour of love for Zoe, and how brilliant it is that it has been shared with us all. It is, quite simply, a triumph.

Stuart Pryke, co-author of *Ready to Teach: Macbeth*

Bringing Forth
the
Bard

A Guide to Teaching Shakespeare
in the English Classroom

Zoe Enser

Crown House Publishing Limited

www.crownhouse.co.uk

First published by
Crown House Publishing Limited
Crown Buildings, Bancyfelin, Carmarthen, Wales, SA33 5ND, UK
www.crownhouse.co.uk

and

Crown House Publishing Company LLC
PO Box 2223, Williston, VT 05495, USA
www.crownhousepublishing.com

First published 2022.

Cover images © Claudio Divizia and coward_lion – stock.adobe.com.

Elizabeth I image, page 34 © Georgios Kollidas – stock.adobe.com.
Needle and thread image, page 104 © Marina – stock.adobe.com.

Quotes from Ofsted and Department for Education documents used in this
publication have been approved under an Open Government Licence. Please see:
http://www.nationalarchives.gov.uk/doc/open-government-licence/version/3/.

British Library Cataloguing-in-Publication Data

A catalogue entry for this book is available from the British Library.

Print ISBN 978-178583629-9
Mobi ISBN 978-178583632-9
ePub ISBN 978-178583633-6
ePDF ISBN 978-178583634-3

LCCN 2022930825

Printed and bound in the UK by
Charlesworth Press, Wakefield, West Yorkshire

Foreword

One of my favourite Shakespeare on-screen cameos comes from the
unlikely place of the Arnold Schwarzenegger movie, *Last Action Hero*.[1]
Young Danny is a boy looking for heroes and he does not find them at
school. When his teacher (played by a pained Joan Plowright) introduces the film version of Hamlet, starring Laurence Olivier, Danny
watches in frustration as the effete Dane thinks about whether to act
and lets his dagger drop limply from his pampered hand. Urging him
'don't talk, just do it', Danny imagines how Hamlet might look if he
really were an action hero. His daydream superimposes Schwarzenegger's
beefy physique onto the moody prince and he watches with delight as
this new testosterone-fuelled Hamlet goes on a killing spree through the
corridors of Elsinore. 'To be or not to be?' the Terminator-tragedian
asks, opting for 'not to be' as he pulls the trigger on his enemies. A voice-
over affirms that 'no one is going to tell this sweet prince goodnight' as
the castle explodes in CGI flames.

As a self-conscious response to Olivier's film, *Last Action Hero* is splen-
did. As a parable of the place of Shakespeare in the classroom, less so.
What Joan Plowright clearly needed was not her classically trained
actor-husband ('You may have seen him as Zeus in *Clash of the Titans*,'
she tells her bored pupils), but rather *Bringing Forth the Bard*. This practical and informative study, written by Zoe Enser, comes from a place of
real love of Shakespeare's works and of experience and commitment in
teaching them. It covers lots of background, critical approaches and
classroom tips, bringing forward content in ways designed to help busy
teachers meet – and generate – students' questions.

I admire the way this book combines openness to interpretation with
clarity about how to work effectively with these texts. It points the way
to a range of resources, many freely available online, from which teachers
can develop their thinking and recharge their love of their subject. And
most refreshing of all, it is not bound by narrow assessment objectives
or reductive frameworks, even as it is astute about what is feasible in real

---

1   *Last Action Hero*, dir. John McTiernan [film] (Columbia Pictures, 1993).

schools with real students. Anyone teaching Shakespeare will find in it stimuli, ideas and reassurance about why it matters.

Emma Smith, Professor of Shakespeare Studies, Hertford College, University of Oxford, and author of *This Is Shakespeare: How to Read the World's Greatest Playwright*

Acknowledgements

This book is dedicated to some of the most important players who have walked the stage with me.

First, Kallum, who came with me to watch some of the most enlivening amateur productions of the Bard's plays I have seen and whose curiosity kept me questioning what was contained within.

Then Dave, whose much-coveted tome of Shakespeare's works enticed me to the bookshelf, just as he tantalised me with ideas of 'all that glisters is not gold'[1] and 'the green-eyed monster', weaving them amongst my childhood fairy tales.

To Pat and Mervyn who, whilst never able to fully join me on this voyage, would never have doubted what it meant to me.

I would also like to thank all those teachers who have contributed to this book by sharing their practice in the case studies, and Emma Smith for her foreword and the valuable insights she always shares in her own work on the Bard.

And finally, for my own spinner of stories, creator of dreams and master wordsmith – Mark:

> 'I love you more than words can wield the matter,
>
> Dearer than eyesight, space and liberty'

(Lear, I, i, 57–58)

---

1   William Shakespeare, *Othello*, in *The Complete Works of William Shakespeare (The Oxford Shakespeare)*, ed. with a glossary by William. J. Craig (Oxford: Oxford University Press, 1916), III, iii, 166. Available at: https://oll4.libertyfund.org/title/craig-the-complete-works-of-william-shakespeare-the-oxford-shakespeare. All further references are to this edition.

Contents

Chronology of Shakespeare's work[1]

The Two Gentlemen of Verona (Two Gent.) (1589–1591)

Henry VI, Part 2 (2 Hen. VI) (1591)

Henry VI, Part 3 (3 Hen. VI) (1591)

Henry VI, Part 1 (1 Hen. VI) (1591–1592)

Titus Andronicus (Tit. A.) (1591–1592)

The Taming of the Shrew (Tam. Shr.) (1590–1591)

Richard III (Rich. III) (1592–1593)

Edward III (1592–1593)

The Comedy of Errors (Com. Err.) (1594)

Love's Labour's Lost (LLL) (1594–1595)

Love's Labour's Won (LLW) (1595–1596)

Richard II (Rich. II) (1595)

Romeo and Juliet (Rom. & Jul.) (1595)

A Midsummer Night's Dream (Mids. N D.) (1595)

King John (John K.) (1596)

The Merchant of Venice (Merch. V) (1596–1597)

Henry IV, Part 1 (1 Hen. IV) (1596–1597)

The Merry Wives of Windsor (Merry W.) (1597)

Henry IV, Part 2 (2 Hen. IV) (1597–1598)

Much Ado About Nothing (Much Ado) (1598–1599)

Henry V (Hen. V) (1599)

Julius Caesar (Jul. Caes.) (1599)

As You Like It (AYL) (1599–1600)

---

1 This chronology is approximate due to the fragmented nature of the surviving plays. Plays such as
Cardenio were attributed to Shakespeare much later (1653), alongside John Fletcher. Work around
authentication and collaboration continues as part of the academic discipline.

Hamlet (*Haml.*) (1599–1601)

Twelfth Night (*Twel. N*) (1601)

Troilus and Cressida (*Tr. & Cr.*) (1600–1602)

Sir Thomas More (1592–1595; Shakespeare's involvement, 1603–1604)

Measure for Measure (*Meas, for M.*) (1603–1604)

Othello (*Oth.*) (1603–1604)

All's Well That Ends Well (*All's Well*) (1604–1605)

King Lear (*Lear*) (1605–1606)

Timon of Athens (*Timon*) (1605–1606)

Macbeth (*Macb.*) (1606)

Antony and Cleopatra (*Ant. & Cl.*) (1606)

Pericles (*Per.*) (1607–1608)

Coriolanus (*Coriol.*) (1608)

The Winter's Tale (*Wint. T.*) (1609–1611)

Cymbeline (*Cymb.*) (1610)

The Tempest (*Temp.*) (1610–1611)

Cardenio (1612–1613), with John Fletcher

Henry VIII (*Hen. VIII*) (1612–1613)

The Two Noble Kinsmen (*Two Noble K.*) (1614–1615), with John Fletcher

The First Folio[1]

The Comedies

The Tempest

The Two Gentlemen of Verona

The Merry Wives of Windsor

Measure for Measure

The Comedy of Errors

Much Ado About Nothing

Love's Labour's Lost

A Midsummer Night's Dream

The Merchant of Venice

As You Like It

The Taming of the Shrew

All's Well That Ends Well

Twelfth Night

The Winter's Tale

---

1   William Shakespeare, *Mr. William Shakespeares Comedies, Histories, & Tragedies. Published According to the True Originall Copies* [The First Folio] (London: Issac and William Jaggard and Edward Blount, 1623); the order of the *First Folio* is included here as it has been influential in terms of how we think of the chronology of Shakespeare and the categorisation of the plays. As you will see, if you compare this to the actual chronology, this can be problematic – especially as readings of plays such as *The Tempest* can be heavily influenced by whether you regard this as one of the first of his plays or his last. There are also some significant omissions such as *Pericles*, *The Rape of Lucrece* and the Sonnets, meaning this is far from a complete compendium, but it has frequently shaped how we think about the development of his writing and which play fits into which category.

The History Plays

King John

Richard II

Henry IV, Part 1

Henry IV, Part 2

Henry V

Henry VI, Part 1

Henry VI, Part 2

Henry VI, Part 3

Richard III

Henry VIII

The Tragedies

Troilus and Cressida

Coriolanus

Titus Andronicus

Romeo and Juliet[2]

Timon of Athens

Julius Caesar

Macbeth

Hamlet

King Lear

Othello

Antony and Cleopatra

Cymbeline

---

2   *Troilus and Cressida* was originally intended to follow *Romeo and Juliet* in this collection but the typesetting was stopped (probably due to a conflict over the rights to the play); it was later inserted as the first of the tragedies, when the rights question was resolved. Therefore, it does not appear in the Folio's table of contents.

Introduction

Regardless of how you personally perceive Shakespeare's work, there is no doubt his appeal and influence is enduring. His plays have been adapted for film many times, with at least 525 listing him in the writing credits.[1] His works are available in print in over 100 different languages, and volumes of his plays and poems dominate many collections.[2] People travel worldwide to visit his birthplace and the famous Globe Theatre, despite the current Globe being a reconstruction of the original where the plays would have been performed, and his plays are studied in the compulsory education system in over 20 countries across the world.[3] A study by the British Council in 2016 found that his popularity is still sky high worldwide, the English national curriculum continues to stipulate the inclusion of two plays for study at Key Stage 3, one at Key Stage 4 and his work continues to be studied at A level in most literature courses.[4] Cinematic productions, such as the wonderfully Bergmanesque production of *Macbeth*, directed by Joel Coen, continue to draw people into his world, breathing new life into words written over four centuries ago.[5]

Whilst he is still prevalent on school curriculums across the globe, the importance of his work goes beyond the school room; Harold Bloom, in his famous exploration of the Bard's work entitled *The Invention of the Human*,[6] explores how Shakespeare shaped the way we think about ourselves and the world around us. Over the centuries we have turned to Shakespeare, as we have other fiction, to seek an understanding of ourselves and in doing so we have come to project some of his ideas onto our everyday lives. Bloom also frequently riffs on Sigmund Freud's obsession with reading Shakespeare, relating this to our collective psyche

---

1   Stephen Follows, 'How many movies based on Shakespeare's plays are there?', *Film Data and Education* (14 April 2014). Available at: https://stephenfollows.com/movies-based-on-shakespeare-plays/#:~:text=Of%20the%20movies%20based%20on,film%20adaptations%20of%20Shakespeare%20plays.
2   See https://www.bbc.co.uk/teach/why-is-the-bard-so-poular-abroad/zhcjrj6.
3   See https://www.bbc.co.uk/teach/why-is-the-bard-so-poular-abroad/zhcjrj6.
4   Mark Brown, 'Shakespeare more popular abroad than in Britain, study finds', *The Guardian* (19 April 2016). Available at: https://www.theguardian.com/culture/2016/apr/19/shakespeare-popular-china-mexico-turkey-than-uk-british-council-survey#:~:text=The%20report%2C%20called%20All%20the,countries%20on%20an%20unprecedented%20scale.
5   *The Tragedy of Macbeth*, dir. Joel Coen [film] (Apple Original, 2021).
6   Bloom, *Shakespeare: The Invention of the Human* (London: Penguin, 2001).

and how this has now supported much of our understanding of the human mind. It seems Freud, another influential thinker in our Western culture, was very much led by Shakespeare's presentation of humanity and Bloom jokingly claims it was not Freud who was reading Shakespeare, but Shakespeare who was reading Freud, and that the 'Freudian map of the mind is (in fact) Shakespeare's'.[7] This gentle mocking aside, what Bloom alludes to here is the notion that Shakespeare's writing has shaped who we are, inventing us, reflecting the concerns, anxieties, loves and complexities of who we are – even as he guides us into being who we are.

References to the Bard have also infiltrated our everyday speech, cropping up in idioms and references which help construct the way we see the world. The British rapper Stormzy even appears to be a fan, crowning himself a troubled king of the Shakespearean ilk with his *Heavy is the Head* album,[8] paraphrasing a line from *2 Henry IV* which reads, 'uneasy lies the head that wears a crown' (III, i, 31).

Fully understanding his oeuvre – with 37 plays, 159 sonnets and four longer poems – is a vast undertaking. To study everything written about Shakespeare's life, world and work is an undertaking which would be even more vast; Bill Bryson anticipates it would take over 27 years just to read what has been written about Shakespeare contained in the Library of Congress (at the rate of one text per day) with the eminent *Shakespeare Quarterly* journal publishing 4,000 new works, including books and studies, every year.[9]

Even just starting to explore the catalogue of work around the Bard is certainly not something the majority of those teaching English in schools would have the time to do and, despite most being English graduates (if their experience was anything like mine), their studies would merely scratch the surface. During my formal education I encountered *Romeo and Juliet* at GCSE, *Twelfth Night* and *Antony and Cleopatra* at A level and a strangely intensive collection of six plays at undergraduate level. My postgraduate studies introduced me to *Coriolanus* and the opportunity to delve into three plays in depth for my dissertation. My own teaching career, spanning over 20 years, saw me teaching only a handful of plays again. His appeal to me has endured, though – starting

---

7   Harold Bloom, *The Western Canon: The Books and School of the Ages* (London: Harcourt, Brace & Co., 1994), p. 25.
8   Stormzy, *Heavy is the Head* (Atlantic Records UK, 2019).
9   Bill Bryson, *Shakespeare: The World as Stage* (New York: Atlas Books, 2007), p. 20.

with marvelling at Mickey Rooney's depiction of Puck in the 1935 version of *A Midsummer Night's Dream*[10] which I stumbled upon one rainy afternoon as a child, and a play which continues to fascinate me in a way that I hope translates to the students I have taught over the years.

Subject knowledge matters

In the current educational climate, having a deep understanding of your curriculum and how it builds over time is key. This also means that thinking deeply about our subject – its different components and what knowledge is important to develop – is of utmost importance if we are to deliver a curriculum that provides all that our students will need in order to become lifelong readers and explorers of English literature. There is an increasing amount of research into the area of continuing professional development (CPD) and what it is that makes it effective. The new *Early Career Framework*,[11] along with the newly developed national professional qualifications programme and the *Initial Teacher Training Core Content Framework*,[12] highlights the need for subject and content knowledge to be a key consideration in teacher development.

The review of international teacher development, commissioned by the Teacher Development Trust and TES Global and conducted by a team from Durham University, CUREE and the UCL Institute of Education, found the research highlighted:

> the equal importance of both pedagogic and subject knowledge. Professional development programmes must consider both subject knowledge and subject-specific pedagogy in order to achieve their full potential. Findings from the strongest review went even

---

10 *A Midsummer Night's Dream*, dir. Max Reinhardt and William Dieterle [film] (Warner Bros. Pictures, 1935).

11 Department for Education, *Early Career Framework* (2019). Available at: https://assets.publishing. service.gov.uk/government/uploads/system/uploads/attachment_data/file/978358/Early-Career_ Framework_April_2021.pdf.

12 Department for Education, *ITT Core Content Framework* (2019). Available at: https://assets. publishing.service.gov.uk/government/uploads/system/uploads/attachment_data/file/974307/ITT_ core_content_framework_.pdf.

further, showing that professional development focussed on generic pedagogy is insufficient, particularly in maths.[13]

However, I would argue that this is just as important in English literature and other humanities subjects too, where the breadth of knowledge required to make significant curriculum decisions and design effective teaching opportunities really challenges teachers to know their content thoroughly. Our students need to be able to develop conceptual responses to his work, which means we need to understand what that means too. We therefore also need to have the opportunity to explore, debate and discuss those texts and ideas we want to include in our curriculum as well as be able to examine how the best approaches apply to that content and our classrooms.

The 2021 Ofsted review of history identifies that effective curriculum choices are not only reliant on the big decisions we make about content, though – and they argue that:

> teachers make additional 'live' curriculum decisions as they teach lessons. The micro-choices they make can add additional detail to their oral storytelling or to particular aspects of source material that they choose to explain and emphasise. This 'live' decision-making by individual teachers is likely to be better judged and managed when underlying rationales for content selection are fully understood and when teachers have had opportunities to regularly discuss content selection and its purposes, as well as the marriage of disciplinary and substantive content.[14]

This suggests that it is not only having knowledge of the already highlighted subject area that is important, but how we hold a deep and broad understanding of the subject, the stories that surround it, as well as the substantive knowledge (the inflexible and immovable facts) and the disciplinary knowledge (how we think about and explore our subject – for example, by taking a particular literary or historical perspective). The more we ourselves know and understand about this topic, the better the position we are in to utilise this in the classroom.

---

13 Teacher Development Trust, *Developing Great Teaching: Lessons from the International Reviews into Effective Professional Development* (2014), p. 20. Available at: https://tdtrust.org/wp-content/uploads/2015/10/DGT-Summary.pdf.

14 Ofsted, *Research Review Series: History* (14 July 2021). Available at: https://www.gov.uk/government/publications/research-review-series-history/research-review-series-history.

Aims of this book

This subject focus is therefore one of the key aims of this book. After my own experiences in teaching his work, I wanted to collate the substantive and disciplinary knowledge around Shakespeare that will help readers to be more effective in the teaching of his plays. What becomes more apparent as we return to his work over the years is the significance of looking at Shakespeare as a topic in itself – not to be confined to individual plays or poems, but as a body of work. Many of the themes and ideas developed over his lifetime and, the complexity that arrives with editorial decisions or arguments regarding additions and omissions aside, there is much to be gained by enhancing your understanding of his work as a whole. Building a detailed schema about his work, his world, his ideas and his influences will enrich how we approach teaching his texts to our students, as well as building our own cultural literacy along the way.

Having spent time studying the breadth of Shakespeare's work, now I could no longer teach students about the intricacies of Lady Macbeth's character without making reference to Shakespeare's other female characters – such as Beatrice from *Much Ado About Nothing* or Portia from *The Merchant of Venice*, who have given me a broader understanding of the role of women in his work – anymore than I could teach it without making reference to her 'the raven himself is hoarse' speech (*Macb.*, I, v, 38–55). Comparing and contrasting his representation of characters and themes can build greater understanding of those ideas, as well as introducing students to the surrounding debates and discussions that allow them to begin to create new and exciting interpretations.

These links across his work, his use of source materials and his influences are important elements to consider in relation to this. The act of *imitatio*, where writers consciously make use of familiar ideas and structures, is a key element of Shakespeare's writing and is deployed freely in his work, both as an exercise in intellectual athleticism – the writer demonstrating their education and academic prowess – and a way in which the audience can take pleasure in spotting cross references and familiar tales. It was a method also deployed by his contemporaries, who drew upon similar source material or revised and reworked their own texts and those of their peers. This isn't a method that would be unfamiliar to modern audiences either; consider the joy derived from spotting our own references to popular culture as we read, or the world-building and crossovers that exist in the Marvel universe or in the work of writers such as Terry Pratchett. What has happened with Shakespeare's writing, though, is that those references have lost some of their resonances with us over time – eroded over the years where we have not been immersed in the theatre and writing of the period. This does not mean we cannot derive pleasure from the plays without it, but there is much to be gained by exploring these crossovers – both for us as teachers and scholars of English literature and our students, who can equally enjoy the experience of seeing connections between stories and writers.

As mentioned before, though, how would English teachers have the time to explore his work in that level of depth? It was certainly not something I would have been able to achieve, especially in my early career or as a head of department. That is why I wanted to write this book. It is an opportunity for teachers to be able to access the information they need in order to enrich their teaching beyond a single play and begin to unpick the threads of his work as a whole, in a way that will enrich their explanation and understanding of the texts. It is an opportunity for them to widen their knowledge – and that of their students, who we want to empower to engage with the ideas and allusions both within and to his work, which remain prevalent throughout much of the English-speaking world.

No precis can act as a substitute for years of high-quality academic study, but this book offers a starting point and a way to quickly access some of the main discussion points around the plays. It introduces some of the most common threads woven throughout his work in relation to his world and context, his themes, his language and the wide variety of performances – and provides a gateway into exploring these in more depth. We, of course, don't need our students to know absolutely everything about the plays they study either (wonderful as that may be), so we need to be selective in what we present and when. The more we know about his work though, the more confident we can be in making those choices for them.

Breaking down barriers

Sometimes the very first hurdle we encounter is, 'Why do we bother to teach Shakespeare at all?' Adults and students hold many misconceptions about his work, thinking of him as an archaic figure and lacking in relevance to our everyday lives. His world, as well as the man as a historical figure, can feel totally removed from our lived experiences and therefore why on earth should we study the work of 'a dead white man'? How can his work be relevant to us today and should we allow this dominance to continue? The world of literature can feel dominated by the likes of Dickens, Wordsworth, Shelley and Shakespeare and there are rightly concerns about who and what may be crowded out of the world of literature by their dominance. This debate continues to appear in many forums, and academics and teachers alike are unable to reach a consensus as to how we might address this. But the inclusion of Shakespeare can still enable us to create diversity. Novels, plays and poems from a wide range of different perspectives continue to discuss the same topics that concerned Shakespeare – and using his work as a conduit can allow us to explore, challenge and question the ideas he presents in his texts, amplifying new voices and experiences as we go. Exploring who is represented, how and, indeed, who is missed out, is an important issue to discuss in our classrooms too.

However, even if we worry about his dominance in our exam specifications, there is always value to be found in his work – something that English teacher Patrick Cragg explores with his students as a starting point to any study of Shakespeare. He outlines his approach in the following case study.

Eventually, one of your students will ask, 'Why are we doing Shakespeare?' How do you answer? How do you explain why one Elizabethan playwright is now a whole subdiscipline in the subject called English? Perhaps you could talk about rich vocabulary and developing critical skills. Perhaps you could talk about the canon and its role in our national identity and academic life. Perhaps, if you're feeling frazzled, you could simply say, 'Because it's in the exam.' The answer I like to give is: 'Because Shakespeare is brilliant, and this is why.'

Teenagers are professionally unenthused, so a good question to ask yourself when you approach a new unit of work is what moments excite you, the teacher, and how you might convey some of that excitement in class. What is it, exactly, that Shakespeare does to you?

The first of those moments arrives for me when our Year 7 pupils study Act II of *A Midsummer Night's Dream*; specifically, Titania's two speeches to Oberon as they argue over the fortunes of a 'little changeling boy' whom Titania possesses and Oberon wants for his own fairy retinue. The first speech, beginning 'These are the forgeries of jealousy', depicts a great upset in the natural world. The fairy king and queen bring down floods, plagues and destruction on a biblical scale. It's the sort of imagery we might find today in a fantasy novel or the second act of a Marvel movie:

> The winds, piping to us in vain,
>
> As in revenge, have suck'd up from the sea
>
> Contagious fogs; which, falling in the land,
>
> Have every pelting river made so proud
>
> That they have overborne their continents

> (*Mids. N D.*, II, i, 88–92)

There may be teachers who can read this without declaiming it (like Cate Blanchett playing Galadriel), or covering the whiteboard in apocalyptic pictures, or diving headlong into creative writing. I am not one of those teachers. But I think Shakespeare really shows his superpowers on the next page, in Titania's second speech, beginning 'His mother was a vot'ress of my order'. Now the fairy queen recounts her friendship with the changeling boy's mother. It's beautiful: an affectionate, funny and wistful account of a friendship between two women:

> Full often hath she gossip'd by my side,
>
> And sat with me on Neptune's yellow sands,
>
> Marking the embarked traders on the flood;

When we have laugh'd to see the sails conceive
And grow big-bellied with the wanton wind

(Mids. N D., II, i, 125–129)

Titania's friend later dies in childbirth, and the speech comes to a moving end:

But she, being mortal, of that boy did die;
And for her sake do I rear up her boy,
And for her sake I will not part with him.

(Mids. N D., II, i, 135–137)

That's the moment, I tell Year 7. Now we're in the presence of greatness, when we see Shakespeare's ability to switch between the widescreen and the close-up, to flip the mood on stage in just a few lines: one moment it's floods and contagious fogs; the next we're sitting by the riverside with two friends, watching the boats go past; and the next we hear Titania's declaration of love and loyalty, fierce in its simplicity. I can understand that friendship. I can picture the trading ships. I can hear Titania's laugh when she jokes about her pregnant friend. I can feel her grief and her protectiveness over the boy.

Keeping up with Shakespeare's plots can be hard; analysing his dense imagery in class can be a slog. So, in those moments when the characters snap into focus, suddenly alive and present, I make sure my students know just how much awe and enthusiasm I think they deserve. They're the best possible answer to why we're doing Shakespeare.

The beauty of what Shakespeare has to offer should not be ignored in favour of more modern or, as some may argue, more relevant texts. Nor should modern texts be shunned in his favour. Instead, the works of Shakespeare can sit beautifully alongside them all, enriching our understanding of the world, and ourselves, and reverberating in its splendour as any work of art would.

That is not to say, of course, it is not difficult to teach – and understanding the plays is a complex enough issue for us as expert readers and expert audiences, let alone those still getting to grips with the English language. However, debating his themes and ideas is part of being involved in the academic world of literature and something which English as a subject in schools has found difficult to engage with. We need to re-enter that debate, though, as part of the joy of exploring Shakespeare's texts is the myriad of interpretations and ideas which emerge with each new visitation. That Shakespeare is still such a mysterious figure to us, and one which students often regard as speaking in riddles, means that there will always be much to discuss and examine. And this is something that I believe is both healthy and important, providing a way into some of the biggest debates about English literature, language, the canon and our understanding of its position in the world. Being able to examine his work – explore it with students and debate meaning, intention and reception – is something that has always brought much pleasure to me in the classroom, and seeing the awe and wonder that students approach these stories with is something that I, and many others, have certainly come to cherish. We also talk in terms of students being able to now explore texts conceptually – and unless we can guide them towards this, analysing our own thinking about the themes and big ideas presented in his work, this will continue to be something they struggle to achieve. We need to model what this looks like in order to lead them into this maze of ideas, but that requires our own engagement beyond simply presenting students with what is on the exam specifications.

Cultural literacy: beyond examinations and pub quizzes

As someone who also came from a background without the advantages of a world of theatre and access to Shakespeare's texts throughout my childhood, entering into the world of Shakespeare and the debates and discussions around it has been both an enriching and empowering experience. We are at a point where the concepts of *cultural capital* and *cultural literacy* are very much at the fore, appearing in the current

Education Inspection Framework and regularly dissected in relation to ideas of *powerful knowledge*.[15]

Again, whilst we might contest Shakespeare's right to his position as powerful in terms of the knowledge studying his plays bring, we need to consider what this might mean for students who come from some of the most deprived backgrounds. Introducing his ideas and language and examining the overall impact of Shakespeare might just be a way in which we can introduce them to a range of conversations that could transform their world view and their opportunities. By examining his influences, allusions, source materials and reach of this work, the young people in our care may well find something that enriches their experience and enables them to engage with the world in a different way. Conversely, they may well leave our classrooms never intending to look at another Shakespeare play and that is entirely their right. But when a politician, a friend or a work colleague makes reference to something from his works, they are in with a chance to meet that on a par with others. They won't be left out of the conversation. The study of great literary texts, be they to your taste or not, is ultimately about providing students with options, and I want all students to have the chance to engage with that regardless of their postcode or parents' financial situation.

Providing them with this opportunity is very much dependent on our own cultural literacy, but often we can be confined by our own experiences and knowledge of literature and the world. It is important, therefore, that we find ways to continually engage with our subject if we wish to transmit this kind of empowering knowledge to our students. We owe it to them to know more and understand where our own ideas have emerged from and to recognise it is more than just an interesting, but quite arbitrary, pub quiz skill to recall who wielded the knife in *Julius Caesar* or recognise an allusion to *King Lear* when talking about a leader in decline.

---

15 Ofsted, *Education Inspection Framework* (updated 19 April 2021). Available at: https://www.gov.uk/government/publications/education-inspection-framework/education-inspection-framework. Michael Young explains that knowledge is powerful 'if it predicts, if it explains, if it enables you to envisage alternatives', Michael Young and David Lambert, *Knowledge and the Future School: Curriculum and Social Justice* (London: Bloomsbury, 2014), p. 74.

Critical lenses

One of the joys of studying Shakespeare is the myriad of ways in which he can be interpreted. Our understanding of his work as we seek to find meaning amongst his language and explore how his characters reflect ourselves back on us, if he is (as Hamlet says) holding 'the mirror up to nature; to show virtue her own feature' (*Haml.*, III, ii, 23–24), is shaped by our understanding of his ideas and world – but equally that of our own. Critical theory, something which has proven to be as protean as the man himself, shifts and changes our understanding with each new lens we apply to his work. But we are not always aware of these influences, especially if we do not teach them directly. I am partial to a psychoanalytical reading of texts, having explored the influence of Freud, Jung and Kristeva on a variety of critical readings.[16] However, I will equally turn my attention to feminist, Marxist and postcolonial interpretations of Shakespeare's plays, happy to move between them to consider a different perspective in my overall analysis. We are not always fully aware of our approaches, though, having become deft in our ability to utilise these at will. But as we are teaching students without this toolkit, it is useful to introduce them to the possibilities these create – as well as being aware of what we ourselves are bringing to the reading, and teaching, of the text.

To summarise some of the most common approaches, including some new lenses which have emerged in recent years, I have listed them below with a brief example of how they might be used.

Marxist

This approach explores the power structures within society, relating to capital and wealth; the inclusion of different classes in his plays, for example, such as the nobility in *Twelfth Night* with the position of characters such as Maria and Feste being very much beholden to the whims of their household leader. Similarly, we can explore why Shakespeare includes characters who are both *high* and *low* in his plays, reflecting on

---

16 Sigmund Freud is often referred to as the father of psychology and, although much of his work is highly problematic (even refuted by many in terms of an understanding of the human mind), his ideas and influence – as much shaped by his own exploration of Shakespeare and other writers, such as E. T. Hoffman – can be an interesting way to read literature. His influence is also felt in the work of theorists such as Carl Jung, building on much of what Freud says in terms of the ego and the id and childhood development, and later critics and philosophers such as Julia Kristeva.

what it may tell us about the power structures that exist between them as well as the world in which they inhabit.

Feminist/gender and queer studies

Shakespeare's obsession with male–female relationships cannot be ignored but he is equally interested in masculinity, femininity and sexuality. Homoerotic overtones are present in some of his closest male relationships, and Sonnet 20 written to the 'fair youth' as well as the 'dark lady' seems to suggest an inner turmoil in the relationship he is presenting between the three. This, alongside other readings of his work, has given speculation to his own attitudes to a more fluid sexuality and his own relationships.

Postcolonialist

Exploring the world from the perspective of power, religion, culture and literature in relation to colonial hegemony. Looking at the character of Caliban in *The Tempest* through this lens is an especially interesting one, as you consider his relationship with Prospero from the perspective of the coloniser and the colonised. The gift of language Prospero bestows on him, whilst at the same time taking ownership of his land and binding others to it – including Ariel – is worth consideration at all key stages.

New historicism and cultural materialism

New historicism is a term coined by Stephen Greenblatt; this approach is a way of examining literature and the world through its cultural context.[17] This means reading works of literature side by side with historical texts as part of the overall discourse. For Shakespeare this means not decoupling his works from the historical period in which they were written, but seeing them as documents related to his period of time. Therefore, when we read plays such as *Romeo and Juliet*, we need to examine them as reflective of the world in which Shakespeare lived and as an embodiment of the values and ideas of the period. This is something we consider a great deal in our classrooms as we create links to the historical period and see the play as embedded in the society in which it was created. This contrasts with approaches such as those of Roland

---

17 John N. King, 'Renewing Literary History' (a review of *The Power of Forms in the English Renaissance*, ed. Stephen Greenblatt), *Shakespeare Quarterly* 35(2) (1984): 237–239 at 237. Available at: https://doi.org/10.2307/2869941.

Barthes, who argues the language has become decoupled from the authorial intent and the layers of meaning come solely from the reader, not the scriptwriter who has merely laid the ground.[18]

Deconstructionist/structuralist

Structuralism is an approach focusing on the use of language and its semiotic power in conveying meaning. It looks closely at what the words signify – for example, the word *red* and its connotations – and draws conclusions around this.

Deconstructionism was a reaction to this – as well as to historicist readings – where literary critics, linguists and philosophers argued about a lack of meaning present in the words and instead examined gaps and silences for new meaning. Rooted in the ideas of Jacques Derrida, it questions some of our most basic assumptions about language and truth and considers how we continue to seek meaning through the text as opposed to finding it.

This can be a compelling approach to some of Shakespeare's plays, as we seek to find a meaning which is rarely an absolute. Hamlet is a character who appears to join us in this quest, constantly striving for an understanding he cannot reach, dismissing language as 'words, words, words' (*Haml.*, II, ii, 196) whilst at the same time being one of the most prolific speakers of Shakespeare's imagination.

Ecocritical

Ecocriticism is a relatively new approach, but interesting when you consider this in the relationship between Shakespeare and the pastoral (discussed later). The use of nature and the idea of the natural world, unbalanced by the interferences of man, is prevalent in a play such as *Macbeth* with the unnatural actions of the protagonists leading not only to destruction of the social order, but the natural one too. In Lennox's description of the wild and chaotic nature of the night of Duncan's death, describing apocalyptic scenes with nature destroying its very self, are clear indicators of how human influences are having a terrifying impact on the world around them (*Macb.*, II, iii, 60–69). Equally, in *King Lear* the storm that whips around them, after Lear's expulsion

---

18 Roland Barthes, 'The Death of the Author'. In *Image-Music-Text*, tr. Stephen Heath (London: Fontana, 1977), pp. 142–148.

from his throne, sets up a discussion about the dialogue between man and nature (*Lear*, III, ii).

Postmodernist

Emerging from the counterculture of the 1950s and 1960s, this approach became dominant in the 1970s onwards – forgoing traditional delineation between high art and popular culture. It is often ironic in approach. It is much indebted to poststructuralism and focuses in on issues such as perceived truths around morality, culture and language, and branched into pretty much all areas of criticism by the 1980s. Criticism of this approach tends to focus on its diversity and its seeming lack of cohesion.

When applied to Shakespeare's work, though, it returns us to the topics of race and gender and deconstructs the language to reveal layers of meaning such as 'old black ram' (*Oth.*, I, i, 88) and 'thick-lips' (*Oth.*, I, i, 66) in *Othello* or descriptions of Shylock in *The Merchant of Venice*.

Postmodern readings place a modern lens upon the texts, not dissimilar to other readings such as feminist or ecocriticism, but perhaps its dominance in the literary world means that we are less likely to recognise its presence as we read his texts.

Animalism

Animalism involves exploring the inclusion of animals within the text – for example, looking at the use of the clown's dog in *The Two Gentlemen of Verona*. Animals can act as a form of another other in this argument and present us with an alternative view of humanity. Emma Smith's brilliant lecture on this in her Oxford podcasts would be highly recommended if you are interested in this approach.[19]

The references to animals and animalistic qualities are also an interesting approach when reading *As You Like It*. The forest of Arden – whilst on the one hand located firmly in our reality, and indeed Shakespeare's, with it being his mother's family name – is shaped into something otherworldly and exotic with the inclusion of snakes and other beasts which would not be as familiar to the audience.

---

19 Emma Smith, 'The Two Gentlemen of Verona', *Approaching Shakespeare* [podcast], University of Oxford (15 December 2017). Available at: https://podcasts.ox.ac.uk/two-gentlemen-verona-0.

Romantic/pastoral

The romantics – such as Wordsworth, Byron and Coleridge – were admirers of Shakespeare, with their appreciation of his poems and plays shaping some of our modern interpretations.[20] For many he was the ultimate creative imagination and his influence can be felt throughout their work, much as it can be felt in the work of Freud. However, much as he inspired their poetry and their readings and interpretations of his writing, he was influential in shaping how we in turn read his work; it is interesting to consider this as a lens that we are perhaps less aware of in terms of how we understand his work.

Coleridge says of him, 'Shakespeare knew the human mind, and its most minute and intimate workings, and he never introduces a word, or a thought, in vain or out of place; if we do not understand him, it is our own fault.'[21] This is an idea that pervades much of our thinking around his writing.

There are various other approaches which have been popular over time, including attempts to read many of Shakespeare's poems and plays as autobiographical in order to find out about the man behind the art. There is little evidence for biographical writing being present during this period, being more closely associated with the advent of the novel form, and despite references to his son, Hamnet, being linked to perhaps his most famous play, *Hamlet*, there is limited evidence suggesting Shakespeare wanted to convey anything about himself in his works. Equally, there are claims that as his parents were Catholics, Shakespeare must be too – but it is not possible to either confirm or deny this from his writing, and theories that Shakespeare must be the character Prospero from *The Tempest* also fall apart once you realise that it was not his last play. The closing words of Prospero are unlikely, therefore, to have been Shakespeare's final farewell to his audience – despite what some readings claim.

Similarly, students can be keen to read characters as autonomous beings filled with desires and motivations beyond the words on the page. This is perhaps exacerbated by Shakespeare's use of historical characters and more than once I have caught students reading a play in an almost biopic

---

20 Joseph M. Ortiz, *Shakespeare and the Culture of Romanticism* (Abingdon: Routledge, 2016).
21 Arthur Symonds, *The Poems of Samuel Taylor Coleridge* (Charleston, SC: BiblioBazaar, 2007), p. 13.

manner. It is always worth making the distinction between the plays as carefully designed works of rhetoric as opposed to autobiographical or biographical documents in which characters are captured as three-dimensional, living and breathing entities beyond the writer, director or actor's reach.

There is, of course, much overlap between the different theories and approaches outlined above and few outside the realms of academia will select just one lens through which to view works of literature. However, it can be empowering for students and teachers alike to step back from their personal readings to consider alternative interpretations that can enrich their understanding. It is also important to remember that, as with any translation and adaptation, the act of approaching texts from a particular historical or critical direction is one of revision. The lens we use and the adaptions we explore will inform how we read the plays, as exemplified in the understanding of the romantics who have shaped our idea of Shakespeare as a creative genius of sublime proportions. But we should continue to strive for students to be able to consider not only their own line of argument but that of those around them, and therefore peering through a range of critical lenses can be a useful method by which we can step outside of ourselves as readers and see a broader picture.

Genre and form

Just as it can be useful to look at Shakespeare via different critical theories, it can be beneficial to explore his writing in terms of genre and form. I can recall being taught that Shakespeare had periods of his life during which he only wrote comedies and only wrote tragedies, with brief forays into the histories and his Roman plays. However, it is not quite so simple, and his choice of form was influenced by not only the classical structures of plays, but also by mystery plays and hybridity, with the tragicomedy as much a part of his repertoire as the forms on their own. Equally, much of our understanding of the sequence of his writing comes from the *First Folio* (see page ix), where the compilers not only organised the plays into three categories (comedy, tragedy and the histories) but also renamed and reordered them, giving rise to a number of misconceptions – especially in relation to his histories which were published here as a historical chronology as opposed to a chronology of writing, performance and publication.[22]

I have also heard some compelling arguments around the idea that *Romeo and Juliet* follows more faithfully the structure of comedy, just one moment and a draught of poison away from a comedic ending. The characters, the secret lovers and the language certainly seem to cast it in quite a different light were it not for that ending, and the rather bleak conclusions for both Malvolio in *Twelfth Night* and Caliban in *The Tempest* cast a dark shadow across those plays which challenges elements of their supposed comedic form.

The chronology included at the front of this book will help to highlight some of the issues around the order of his work, listing them in order of composition as opposed to genre, and this will perhaps help us consider those connections across his texts and where and how he employed the familiar traditions of the theatre. This will be especially important as we consider the intertextuality of the plays, how far they stand alone as individual stories and how far they are part of the same web of narratives.

Tragedy and comedy

The forms of tragedy and comedy were established well before Shakespeare was writing and performing. The conventions of theatre were established in the amphitheatres of ancient Greece: huge affairs, bringing the people together in vast festivals of performance which included dance and song as well as drama. The concept of catharsis and the role of the theatre as a method by which to challenge and explore the key concerns of the community were highlighted in these extravaganzas with the chorus guiding and probing our understanding of who we are, our role within the world and our relationships with the gods as they danced before us.

Shakespeare's tragedies tended to focus on the fall of the princes, which, whilst it does not mean his central tragic heroes need to be literal princes (Hamlet being an obvious exception), they do need to be high-born or

---

22 The *First Folio* is a collection of Shakespeare's works, published after his death in 1623. This collated 36 plays and only 750 copies were produced. Nineteen of his plays had previously been printed in *Quarto* format, but the *First Folio* is considered the most reliable in terms of the content of his plays.

of high standing. Much like the archangel who fell, the good and the bad equally hurtle towards their doom – their *hamartia* exposed to all but themselves until it is too late; hamartia is the fatal flaw that plagues our heroes and leads to their ultimate downfall. Ambition, greed, lust, lack of insight and pride are all traits which lead to the fall of characters throughout our stories.

One simple definition of tragedy involves inevitability. The characters move inexorably towards their demise, with little free will leading them there. As Romeo cries 'O! I am Fortune's fool' (*Rom. & Jul.*, III, i, 142) he, like other tragic heroes, realises that he is caught within his own predetermined fate. The prologue at the start of the play ensures we are never in any doubt as to how this will conclude, and it could be argued there is some comfort in this as we are aware from the start how this is going to end; there is no reason to resist the flow of the plot, which is flowing freely towards a known ending.

Comedy, however, as Susan Snyder argues, is instead defined by *evitabil-ity*[23] instead of a move towards a conclusion which is already defined. Comedies are mutable, with multiple possibilities and opportunities presented to the characters. It means the plays are rollercoaster rides, chaotic and impossible to predict, with the audience eagerly following the twists and turns of the plot.

Most simplistically, of course, we talk in terms of tragedies all ending in death and comedies all ending in marriage and many of Shakespeare's plays fall comfortably within this. All are wed and happy at the end of *A Midsummer Night's Dream, Much Ado About Nothing, Twelfth Night, All's Well That Ends Well* and many others.

However, some plays do not fall so neatly into these boundaries and the tragicomedy blurs these lines. *Measure for Measure*, whilst appearing in the comedy section of the Folio, has been described as tragicomedy, satire and allegory over the years. *Twelfth Night* does not end with marital bliss and harmony for Malvolio (slinking off in his humiliation). Equally, although it ends in death, *Othello* often brings frustration to its audience as Iago fails to get the punishment he truly deserves for his crimes. It seems that even clear categorisation is something that Shakespeare evades with his form, as well as his life and his attitudes.

23 Susan Snyder, *The Comic Matrix of Shakespeare's Tragedies: Romeo and Juliet, Hamlet, Othello, and King Lear* (Princeton, NJ: Princeton University Press, 1979), p. 395.

How to use this book

So, to clarify, this book is not:

+ A guide to breaking down or covering exam board assessment objectives or how to maximise marks.

+ A series of lesson resources and activities for your students.

+ A method of developing a separate pedagogy for Shakespeare, as the principles of effective teaching are going to be much the same as those you will use to successfully teach Dickens, Duffy or Morrison. Making use of questioning to check understanding, probe thinking and encourage application of knowledge is essential. The same is true of the use of retrieval to embed learning and increase fluency of recall, modelling how we talk and write about his work and introducing material in accessible, exciting and challenging ways. These remain an important component of whatever you are teaching and Shakespeare doesn't require something different from these tried and tested methods.

+ A substitute for detailed study of the themes, language and ideas in the specific play you happen to be studying with your students. There are some fantastic books which already do this and the further reading and resources collected at the back of the book will support you to access these.

This is, however, a book which aims to link together the golden threads that run across Shakespeare's work, highlighting where you could explore these with students or include them on your wider English curriculum. This is also a book that will provide some tips and approaches to application of this knowledge in the classroom, taken from a teacher's perspective which can then be examined in relation to your own contexts to deepen students' understanding of the plays they are studying and the overall body of work to which they belong. The case studies from teachers, covering Key Stage 1 to Key Stage 5, provide further opportunities for you to reflect on how you are approaching this and how you might make use of the methods they employ.

But most importantly, this is a book that aims to make clear the links between understanding the subject content to give you an opportunity to think deeply about the subject and how it relates to your curriculum and to support you to see how developing this further can help young people to engage with important works of literature which continue to stand the test of time. It highlights further reading and texts to support the study of his work and will hopefully lead you, and your students, off on some adventures to explore the ideas and themes further.

My main advice for anyone studying the plays with students, though, would be to read the play and read it again. Think about elements like context, language and direction yourself and immerse yourself in the play as much as possible. However, this would be my advice for pretty much any other literary text; unless we have strong subject knowledge ourselves and have challenged our own ideas, misconceptions and inter-pretations, we are unlikely to be able to support our students to understand his work well.

Of course, any writer would be telling a white lie if they didn't say they wanted their reader to devour their book cover to cover, exploring the emerging ideas with a fervour as they leap to the next one. However, I am also very keen for there to be a practical element to this book, so I have included quick links to key plays in the index at the back and sug-gested approaches to the topics to help you to navigate through the texts at a glance. After all, this is intended for those incredibly busy teachers who are trying to juggle so many things over the course of their day.

Hopefully, later you will want to come back for more – maybe even devouring it page by page, making an author very happy in their endeavour.

Chapter 1

Bringing Forth His World

Context, Influences and Inspirations

A plague upon you, murderers, traitors all!

(*Lear*, V, iii, 272)

Why teach it?

The world Shakespeare presents to us can often feel quite remote from our modern perspective, located at a time when things seem alien to our own everyday lives and experiences. Whilst this means immersing ourselves in his stories can provide something of a welcome relief – an escape from reality, as with all fiction – for many of our students this can be a significant barrier. To them the noughties can feel like more lifetimes ago than they can begin to imagine, and the Elizabethan and Jacobean periods may as well be on the moon. This, further compounded by the seemingly impenetrable language, can lead to a perfect storm of confusion.

There are also many misconceptions about his world that have been embedded by popular media, our merging and shifting understanding in the historical or literary world, or even by partially understood snippets of history that have pervaded our society. A quick google brings up questions such as, 'Did Shakespeare know Queen Victoria?', 'Did all men wear tights in Shakespeare's time?' and 'Did they all speak like this?' Students have even had the audacity to wonder if I had met him! All students will have heard of him, but his world, his writing and his importance are wrapped up within cultural understanding of what these were as opposed to the historical or literary truth insofar as we can understand it. This makes it all the more important that we devote some time to exploring context with our students. This will also enrich their understanding of his characters, themes and language and hence why I am starting here in Chapter 1 of this book.

What is it?

As I have mentioned elsewhere, whenever we start to teach about context we run the risk of our lessons becoming history ones, moving away from the disciplinary exploration of literature and into a whole new discipline. Whilst we may have a lot of knowledge about this domain in relation to literature, many of us are not historians and as we strive to ensure students have a good grounding in context, we potentially run the risk of offering something which is an unsatisfying hybrid of the two areas. Context is important though, providing a frame on which to hang his work – just as it is important to understand other contexts in which writers are producing their work. Knowledge of society and women during the early 1800s helps us to contextualise the writing of Austen or Brontë and having knowledge of The Great Depression and the impact of the Dust Bowl in 1930s America helps us to locate the ideas that Steinbeck aimed to address in his novels. However, we always read their texts with fresh eyes, shaped by our own understanding of the world and it is important we don't eclipse new and personal interpretation by overloading a text with context. But an awareness of why certain language is used, some of the specific concerns of the period in which it was written and how they reflected the perspective of the author is still a necessary part of our work if we want students to really understand the text. Imagine, for example, teaching *The Crucible* with no reference to McCarthyism, or Blake's *London* without nods to the French Revolution. Whilst an understanding could be reached, there would be much lost if you didn't have some of these contextual details to hand.

However, finding where the context crosses over into the work, enriching our understanding and helping to shape meaning is a useful approach, so this chapter explores some of the most significant issues that were relevant to Shakespeare's writing and audience. This selection is by no means exhaustive but it provides a framework upon which an understanding of the context can grow as you explore the plays and the context in action.

The theatre and the publishing world

Whilst the Globe has become known for its association with Shakespeare's plays, with many indeed performed there (both during his lifetime and beyond), there were lots of other theatres and venues used too. It is believed that *Julius Caesar* was his first to be performed at the Globe in 1599, with 13 of his 37 plays already having been performed elsewhere. Private performances in courts and taverns were also well established; something we see in both *Hamlet* and *A Midsummer Night's Dream*. Players had traditionally been nomadic troupes and professional actors associated with theatres were a relatively new construct. Much is often made of the open-air nature of the performances at the Globe and there are certainly compelling arguments we could make that suggest this setting is reflected in his work, with language cues as to the time of day and weather which would not have been possible to emulate. However, we need to be cautious not to embed misconceptions around this that could be unhelpful to students' understanding of the plays and performance, just as we should be cautious to suggest they were only ever written for performance.

Nevertheless, when considering the context Shakespeare was working within, the social and political position of theatre and the purpose of the plays is always an interesting area in which to delve. Control of social commentary was linked closely to control of the printed word and it is frequently argued that Shakespeare is a writer eager to challenge the political and social status quo. Whether this is actually the case, as opposed to providing an outlet for some of the anxieties of the period – for example, by exploring concerns around lineage – is very much up for debate. Leonard Tennenhouse argues, 'If art and politics define the same domain of truth when Shakespeare wrote, we must assume his art was always political and it is our modern situation and not his world which prevents us finding his politics on the surface.'[1] If this is the case, then having an awareness of the political context of Shakespeare's writing would certainly enable us to have a deeper understanding of his plays and the themes and ideas he was keen to explore. This is not to say that all his work is subversive or necessarily inviting debate, with much in his work suggesting that hierarchies are upheld – with rightful kings back on the throne and social order restored. The same is true with his

---

1   Leonard Tennenhouse, 'Strategies of State and Political Plays'. In Jonathan Dollimore and Alan Sinfield (eds.), *Political Shakespeare: New Essays in Cultural Materialism* (Manchester: Manchester University Press, 1985), pp. 109–128 at 125–126.

comedies which end in marriage and social harmony is the prevailing message.

But regardless of whether we think Shakespeare was a political animal or not, aiming in his writing to challenge or endorse the status quo, one thing is clear: during his lifetime theatres and publishing were subject to much scrutiny, not least from the diktats of Queen Elizabeth I. In 1581 a decree was passed stating all plays needed to be submitted to the Master of the Revels prior to performance to monitor them for religious or political sedition.[2] This was extended to all publications in 1607 and we know that some of Shakespeare's plays, such as *Richard III* and *Henry IV (Parts 1 and 2)*, were subject to censorship under this ruling. *Richard II* contains a scene in which Richard is deposed (*Rich. II, IV, i*). After the Earl of Essex's unsuccessful revolt against Elizabeth in 1601, the queen complained that a 'certain play' had been performed publicly to encourage insurrection.[3] It was on the eve of the rebellion that Essex's followers had sponsored Shakespeare's company – the Lord Chamberlain's Men – to perform this play and Elizabeth, it seems, saw a clear connection between the two. The censor judged the deposition scene to be too politically sensitive to be performed and it was omitted from all editions of the play until 1608, after Elizabeth's death.

This may have had a significant influence on the work of many play-wrights of the period, and Shakespeare's use of fantastical locations – as in *Twelfth Night, As You Like It* or *The Tempest* – could have enabled Shakespeare freedom of political expression where the histories did not. By removing them from the known locations, he had a licence to satirise and allegorise events taking place in the world around him. In 'Political Propaganda and Satire in *A Midsummer Night's Dream*' Edith Rickert states 'in the years immediately preceding *A Midsummer Night's Dream*, political satire on the public stage was commonplace'[4] – part of the expectation of what the experience would bring. By employing a histor-ical setting, Shakespeare may have been awarded greater licence to navigate the censors, as we see in *Macbeth* or the Roman plays. Students often wonder how he was able to present some of his criticisms of king-ship at a time when political control was at such a height. They assume

---

2   Gary B. Goldstein, 'Did Queen Elizabeth Use the Theatre for Social and Political Propaganda?', *The Oxfordian* VII (2004): 161. Available at: https://shakespeareoxfordfellowship.org/wp-content/uploads/Oxfordian2004_Goldstein-Propaganda.pdf.
3   Ellen Castelow, 'Shakespeare, Richard II and Rebellion', *Historic UK* (n.d.). Available at: https://www.historic-uk.com/HistoryUK/HistoryofEngland/Shakespeare-Richard-II-Rebellion/.
4   Edith Rickert, 'Political Propaganda and Satire in *A Midsummer Night's Dream*' II, *Modern Philology* 21(2) (1923): 133–154.

that this would have made him unpopular in court, whereas in actual fact he was able to explore some of the concerns of the period around power relatively unfettered. Having a greater understanding of how he presented these ideas, both through setting and language, can enrich students' readings of the plays.

Religion, the theatre and censorship – the bishop's law

Censorship did not just involve the political, and religious materials were also subject to the same regulations enforced on fiction and performance. The distinction between the political and the religious during this period and the reformation of the church in England began with Henry VIII in 1534, when he passed a law to make the monarch the Supreme Head of the Church of England. This stemmed in part from the pope's refusal to agree to Henry's request to divorce his wife, but there were also political considerations – particularly involving ownership and power.[5] What this meant for Shakespeare was that he was living at a time when there were significant tensions between the Protestant and Catholic Churches and significant reforms to the publication and distribution of the Bible. Versions of the Bible were removed from publication, once again shaping how his ideas were presented. It is widely accepted that Shakespeare studied the Geneva Bible as that is the one whose wording fits most closely with his own references.[6] Its portability made it popular at the time and was produced by Protestant exiles living in Switzerland. It was also conveniently divided in a way which highlighted key quotes that could be easily sourced and quoted. However, it was likely Shakespeare also had access to the Bishop's Bible and the Book of Common Prayer – and biblical allusions appear in abundance across Shakespeare's writing that align with the language of different publications, suggesting that he was well versed in more than one version.[7]

5 Brian Cummings, 'The Reformation in Shakespeare', *British Library* (15 March 2016). Available at: https://www.bl.uk/shakespeare/articles/the-reformation-in-shakespeare.
6 See https://www.bl.uk/collection-items/the-geneva-bible-1570#:~:text=There%20are%20many%20 Biblical%20references,often%20closest%20to%20this%20text.
7 J. M. Pressley, 'Biblical Shakespeare', *Shakespeare Resource Centre* (n.d.). Available at: https://www. bardweb.net/content/ac/shakesbible.html.

Plague and disease

A plague o' both your houses

(*Rom. & Jul.*, III, i, 111)

If you search on the Open Source Shakespeare website, you will find the word *plague* appears in some form or other in Shakespeare's plays 117 times. It is a particular favourite of Falstaff (used to curse those he does not like) but appears anywhere from *King John* to *Venus and Adonis*. The plague and notions of judgements in the form of disease and pestilence have clear biblical origins, so it is important to acknowledge this too; in Luke 21:11[8] it says there will be plagues, and both Ezekiel and Jeremiah speak of God sending plagues, for example, in Ezekiel 14:21 and 33:27 and Jeremiah 21:6–9.

However, plagues were not something that merely evoked an older time or a wrathful god, but a reality for the people living in England in the 16th century. The resonance felt by an audience seeing whole communities besieged by bubonic plague, and indeed other diseases such as syphilis and smallpox, can't be underestimated. When Falstaff repeatedly references the plague, crying 'A plague upon you all! Give me my horse, you rogues; give me my horse, and be hanged.' (*1 Hen. IV*, II, ii, 33–34), or Mercutio curses both families (*Rom. & Jul.*, III, i, 111), sealing their fate with his dying words, the audience would have felt the impact of those words perhaps more than some subsequent audiences did.

Theatres were subject to closure at the request of privy councils, in their attempts to control the spread of the plague and other diseases. However, theatres were not only seen as sites which carried the risk of the spread of physical disease, but also as places of questionable morality with close links between physical illness and moral impropriety remaining closely linked well into the 1900s. Players and their troupes were regarded as outcasts, liable to bring moral decline through the promotion of their questionable actions and subversive messages, meaning theatres were also under threat from puritanical concerns. One preacher, Thomas White, went so far as to make a direct link between plays and the plague, arguing 'The cause of plague is sinne ... and the cause of

---

8   Robert Carroll and Stephen Prickett (eds.), *The Bible Authorised King James Version* (Oxford: Oxford University Press, 1997). Further references are to this edition.

sinne are plays: therefore, the cause of plagues are plays.'[9] Shutting down the theatres was a real risk to the livelihoods of actors and writers, and it was unlikely the players would have been able to return to their previous lives, once again leading to them taking to a life on the road, reinforcing their status as outsiders and vagabonds. Hamlet says of them:

> O! there be players
>
> that I have seen play, and heard others praise, and that highly, not to
>
> speak it profanely, that, neither having the accent of Christians, nor
>
> the gait of Christian, pagan, nor man, have so strutted and bellowed
>
> that I have thought some of nature's journeymen had made men and
>
> not made them well, they imitated humanity so abominably.
>
> (*Haml.*, III, ii, 33–39)

Despite Shakespeare's success and the enduring nature of theatre, they were not held in high esteem by many at the time.

Shakespeare's contemporaries and collaborators

There has been much debate over the years as to the authorship of Shakespeare's plays. There is often an element of *got you* about revelations that perhaps his work is not exclusively his own. However, collaboration amongst writers was common and, in fact, a well-established practice, and *The Two Noble Kinsmen* and *Henry VIII* were very open collaborations with John Fletcher. He also worked with Thomas Middleton, and scholarship has found much evidence of the conscious sharing of different sections of the plays. This has often caused some head-scratching around the role of Hecate in *Macbeth* (Act III, sc. v), seeming not to fit with the overall structure and focus of the play – as well as there being linguistic differences. Some believe that this was a later addition, but it is equally possible that it is merely further evidence of the collaborative nature of the theatre. There is much to be

---

9   See https://beguidedbyart.com/a-plague-on-both-your-houses/.

gained by exploring not only the work of Shakespeare as a body but that of his contemporaries, where there is greater understanding of the concerns of the period as well as their presentation in a range of forms, as there are many parallels. Some key writers to explore are:

+ Christopher Marlowe; most notably his *Dr Faustus*, which has parallels with those plays of Shakespeare that deal with the fall of Satan.

+ Thomas Kyd, whose *Spanish Tragedy* was hugely influential in the development of Hamlet.

+ John Fletcher, who not only worked closely with Shakespeare but also revised his work later and even wrote a sequel to *The Taming of the Shrew* called *The Tamer Tamed*.

+ Thomas Middleton, who is believed to have collaborated with Shakespeare on *Timon of Athens*, but also for revisions of his work. He is also the author of *The Changeling* and despite not being accredited and much debate around it, it is now widely agreed he was the author of *The Revenger's Tragedy*.

+ Ben Johnson, a playwright and poet perhaps best known for *The Alchemist*, was critical of Shakespeare at times, but three years after his death wrote 'I loved the man, and do honour his memory on this side idolatry as much as any.'[10] Robert Giroux, in the *New York Times*, wrote, 'In 1598 Shakespeare had given him a much-needed helping hand with *Every Man in His Humour*' and there was both rivalry and admiration between the two.[11]

This has only once again scratched the surface of the issues and there are many other considerations regarding context that we need to explore in relation to his texts – for example, understanding some of his depictions of love and marriage which may put Juliet's mother's attitude to her refusal to marry into perspective (marriage as security at an unstable time, as opposed to an individual choice related to love). Equally, some contextual points will have an important resonance when teaching particular plays – the 1606 Gunpowder Plot in relation to *Macbeth*, for instance – and identifying where these topics seem to be shaping the work can be useful when ensuring students understand both the

---

10 Ben Jonson, 'De Shakespeare Nostrat'. In H. Morley (ed.), *Discoveries Made upon Men and Matter and Some Poems* [ebook] (Project Gutenberg, 2014 [1892]). Available at: https://www.gutenberg.org/files/5134/5134-h/5134-h.htm.

11 Robert Giroux, 'The Man Who Knew Shakespeare', *New York Times* (13 February 2000). Available at: https://archive.nytimes.com/www.nytimes.com/books/00/02/13/bookend/bookend.html?_r=1.

playwright and his audience. However, we need to think carefully about how our selections can enrich the readings we want our students to consider and what it means for their understanding of the plays.

How to teach it

Giving students some grounding in what Shakespeare's world was like and providing a sense of where he sits within our history is useful when teaching the plays. There are many misconceptions about what life was like then and I often start by checking these with an introduction in Year 7, then coupling this with an opportunity to explore some of the historical and literary chronology in which a particular work sits. Making use of images or descriptions of Shakespeare's world can be a useful starting point for this. However, most of the time I focus on exploring the context as we begin to unpick the themes, language and structural choices. For example, when I am looking at elements of theatre which may be relevant to his choice of language, such as references to lighting, I will highlight this here. I don't front-load details such as these but weave them into the study of the text.

Equally, when I begin to explore the character of Lady Macbeth or women generally in his writing, it provides a perfect opportunity to talk about the issues which surrounded having a queen as the head of state and the head of the Church. Our students have a very different understanding of the monarchy than Shakespeare and his peers did and have lived their entire lives with a queen on the throne. However, her role is quite different in our modern society. Presenting them with the speech Queen Elizabeth gave to the troops at Tilbury in 1588 where she says 'I know I have the body but of a weak and feeble woman; but I have the heart and stomach of a king, and of a king of England too',[12] provides a different perspective to consider a character who seems to want to reject her femininity and talks of how she would 'shame to wear a heart so white' (*Macb.*, II, ii, 65–66) as her husband quails at his own actions.[13] Although King James is on the throne when *Macbeth* is first performed in 1606, the concerns around gender and leadership remained prevalent in the minds of both the writer and the audience.

12 See https://www.bl.uk/learning/timeline/item102878.html.
13 Further details of Queen Elizabeth's speech and her presentation as a leader and a woman can be found here: https://www.rmg.co.uk/stories/topics/queen-elizabeth-speech-troops-tilbury.

Contextual understanding also includes an awareness of not only Shakespeare's world, but his influences and how he used allusion to classical and well-known stories – as well as considering how his audience may have responded to these elements. For example, when we consider the Prologue in *Romeo and Juliet* there are several contextual points to reflect upon, especially as students will have taken delight in both avoiding and providing spoilers for popular stories; which English teachers still have a class set of *Of Mice and Men* that remains unadorned with that immortal scrawling on the first page which aims to give the game away?

First, the use of the prologue was not only a method to introduce the audience to the play's themes and characters, but as a way of signalling to theatregoers that the show was about to begin; a linguistic version of the theatre bell or *lights down*, if you will. It was also typical of plays during this period, with a significant number of the plays performed in the 1590s including a prologue. By 1620 this seemed to have gone out of fashion and appeared in fewer and fewer new plays performed during this period. However, Shakespeare was working within an accepted framework for the drama performed at this time, and for most of the audience a prologue would have been an expected part of their trip to the theatre. Of course, there is then the issue around the way in which the prologue here does not just introduce the action about to unfold, but deliberately provides a frame in which our story will evolve. We know exactly what will happen before we even have a chance to see who the characters are, and students tend to see this as deflating as opposed to as a gateway into the action the viewer is already well-versed in. If we consider this in relation to the idea of inevitability in tragedy, by setting out the perimeters immediately, the audience is positioned comfortably to watch the tragedy unfold, waiting for the inevitable but knowing they cannot effect change. There is tension, but this is not where the tension arises from.

Although the story of something like *Romeo and Juliet* is familiar, Shakespeare is also framing how his version of the play will be presented. Whilst there are similarities to the other versions of the story, such as *Tristan and Isolde*[14], this is his language, his interpretation and exploration of the story and his characters and he takes ownership of this right from the start. It is no different when I begin to teach the plot

---

14 *Tristan and Isolde* is a well-known chivalric romance, retold many times since the 12th century. It tells of the adulterous love between the Cornish knight, Tristan, and his ward – the Irish princess, Isolde.

of *Romeo and Juliet* in a secondary school, though. I am also starting from a position where most of the story and characters are already known, with many popular versions of the tale still in existence – even animated ones such as *Gnomeo & Juliet*[15] – so I will often spend some time finding out what the students know and checking for any misconceptions which may become a sticking point later if not addressed now (they weren't garden gnomes, for example, and the nurse wasn't a frog). But this wasn't particularly different with the audience of Shakespeare; not only would they have already heard tales of doomed lovers, kept apart – with *Pyramus and Thisbe* (see Chapter 3 on Shakespeare's influence and allusion) – but they will already have heard some of the source material. The plot of the play was taken from a popular poem called *The Tragicall Historye of Romeus and Iuliet*, written by Arthur Brooke and published in 1562. This was reprinted a number of times, suggesting a positive reception.[16] This was only one of the retellings of the story, however, with Italian versions written by Luigi da Porto in the 1530s and Matteo Bandello in the 1550s. A French version was written by Pierre Boaistuau in 1559, once again suggesting that the plot details revealed in the prologue were less about spoiling the ending of the play but locating it in the popular culture of the period. What is significant, of course, is not what Shakespeare is presenting here, but how it is being presented once we are aware that this would be a story already known to the audience. Exploring this with your students is an effective way to encourage them to think about audience, context and authorial intent.

However, when teaching *The Tempest*, I often step back and allow students to explore the character of Caliban without comment. Once they have already spent some time considering his role and his actions, as presented in the text – understandably horrified at his attack on Miranda and wholly sympathetic to Prospero's dominance over such a dangerous creature – I then introduce some points in relation to colonialism, including some exploration of the name *Caliban* in relation to the word *cannibal*, having been synonymous with *indigenous* at the point Shakespeare was writing. We then look at alternative depictions of the character and then return to the lines in the text. Often these take on a new meaning, and whilst discussions around colonialism run much deeper than simple discussions on the Key Stage 3 English curriculum,

---

15 *Gnomeo & Juliet*, dir. Kelly Asbury [film] (Touchstone Pictures, 2011).
16 More details of how the poem compares with Shakespeare's version can be found here: https://www.bl.uk/collection-items/brookes-romeus-and-juliet.

this certainly highlights how these contextual points can be important as we examine a text.

In the following case study, head of English and author Chris Curtis explores how he rather imaginatively teaches aspects of context through the lens of clothing and fashion:

Keeping up with the Tudors; phwoar, look at her high forehead!

For years, exam boards have moaned about bolt-on context in students' responses and how students use any opportunity to throw in spurious historical facts. How to teach context has always been a challenging aspect; fusing contextual knowledge with analysis is really hard to do, let alone teach. The problem lies in the knowledge and the types of knowledge. For me, the answer has relied on contextual understanding rather than contextual knowledge. Students who understand the context reflect this better in their analysis than the students who know contextual knowledge. There's very little you can do with knowing that the play was written in 1595, apart from stating it numerous times in an essay, but there's a lot you can say about the fashion for men carrying swords and daggers around with them. Why did they carry them? How would they be viewed if they didn't carry a sword around with them? Understand this and you understand how Elizabethans viewed men and violence, so when you explore *Romeo and Juliet* you understand why the characters behave in the way they do. And a lot of it is to do with fashion.

Fashion is at the heart of a lot of contextual understanding. Understand the fashion and you understand the context. What was in vogue? What wasn't in vogue? Students do *get* fashion and they understand the complexity and the nuances and issues surrounding it. That's why I always start with paintings of Elizabeth I.[17]

I draw students' attention to her incredibly high forehead. Usually, I ask them if they know why she had such a high forehead. We get the usual thing about wigs – which is partly accurate. Then I explain to them how it was the fashion of women, at the time, to have a high forehead and how it was so desirable that they'd even shave the top of their hairline just so they can have a massive *slap head*. Cue students saying they wouldn't do anything so stupid. At this point, a discussion on previous fashion trends spills into the lesson; thick eyebrows, contouring, skin bleaching, hair straightening, hair dyeing. And so on. If I am brave enough, I might even share my past fashion choices (curtains, spiky hair and a rat's tail, shell suits) or ask them about their parents' fashion choices. We even explore how fashion is different for men and for women. We discuss the reasons behind their choices.

Next, I ask students to consider what they think about how the common Elizabethan people reacted to the Queen's high forehead. Then, we get to a discussion on how celebrities and influencers affect fashion and what the average person did in their day-to-day life.

Once you have the idea clear in their heads about fashion, they get a better understanding of the world and the time. Their parents behaved, dressed and acted largely because of the time. Fashions change. Quickly. Constantly. All too often, students relate Shakespeare's stories to their own time and the way they see the

---

17 See https://www.natgeokids.com/uk/discover/history/monarchy/elizabeth-i-facts/.

world and that's problematic because they miss out on the subtleties of the time.

Approaching the text's context becomes easier when students have the conceptual understanding of fashion and you have a skeleton to work with. You can now, in your teaching, attach bits to it:

- The fashion for carrying a sword, copying Europeans and Italians.
- Mercutio's insults about Tybalt link to the concept of a *fop* (a man too concerned with his fashion).
- The fashion for street fights in Elizabethan England.
- The fashion for a man to have a male lover until they marry.
- The new fashion of marrying for love rather than for status and position, as highlighted by the puritanical elements of society.
- The anti-Catholic sentiment dictated by the monarch of the time – but English history flits between pro- and anti-Catholic sentiment.

By students having a clear understanding of the transient nature of fashion, they can understand its complexity better. It isn't a case of context overload, but a reasoned understanding. Rather than spewing hundreds of facts, they can reason why something happened and the factors influencing it. Take Mercutio's insult about Tybalt: 'the very butcher of a silk button' (*Rom. & Jul.*, II, iv, 23); we have Tybalt being mocked because he is seen by Mercutio as being too obsessed with fashion. This story is debatable. Mercutio is suggesting that he is so weak as a result of his foppish obsession that he hasn't developed or practised his fencing like a typical man. The whole part goes to prove that fashion is a double-edged sword. Fashion has made, in Mercutio's eyes, Tybalt weak. There is a complex relationship between masculinity and fashion; men have to be fashionable, but not too fashionable as it can remove their masculinity. Why are you wearing a sword? For fashion? Or for a fight? The whole thing can add so much depth when explored further:

- Why can't men be obsessed with fashion?
- What would happen to men if they were not fashionable?

⁕ Why isn't there a female version of a fop?

Along the way students can construct the rules governing the fashion or concept. What is allowed? What isn't allowed? They are then able to see what the typical view of the time was and what happens if you break the rules and challenge expectations. I would go on to introduce a text around the idea and help students build up their understanding as they have a grounded understanding of the trend, what happened if you didn't follow the trend and why the trend existed. All too often, we aren't selective with the contextual knowledge we impart. We tend to give a sheet to students with lots of contextual information, when it is easier and more productive, from my experience, to look at a societal rule or current fashion. By exploring that one narrow thread, you can link to gender, religion, politics, class and wealth as you unpick the reasoning behind the rule or fashion.

As you can see in Chris's approach, he encourages students to first relate aspects of context to their world before they begin to reflect on what this might mean for the audience in Shakespeare's time. Once they have reached this understanding, they are then in a better position to explore the choices Shakespeare was making with his language, his setting and his characters. Who knew a forehead could reveal so much? However, what is important is that context doesn't just become an add-on and the links to the historical and social factors reinforce understanding and not detract from it.

Laura Webb, a head of English and self-professed lover of Shakespeare, explains her approach here:

Shakespeare's stories hold their own without context, but I fundamentally believe that the precise introduction of context is key to improve students' understanding of the mechanics of Shakespeare's plays. However, context should never be a bolt-on, tagged on to the start of a unit or mentioned at the end of the play. Effectively teaching context involves weaving it within the teaching of the text, drawing students' attention to key moments and contemporaneous expectations or reactions. It also means remembering that context isn't solely historical; it is worth considering societal issues, dramatic contexts, gender norms, political shifts – context should not be reduced to dates and statistics (which often become tagged on in students' essays, irrelevant to the idea they are exploring).

When teaching *Macbeth* to a group of students targeting the highest grades and moving beyond GCSE, it is the stories I begin with. But then, when we first encounter Duncan and his decision to make Malcolm the Prince of Cumberland, we might discuss what it means to be a monarch in 1606. I would tell students that *Macbeth* was a play written for King James – and then probe their knowledge of the Gunpowder Plot. When we hear about Macbeth's letter to his wife, and him calling her his *partner*, we might discuss how attitudes to gender have evolved over the centuries. These are initial discussions to gauge the level of understanding and then add to it, offering more clarity relevant to that moment in the text. The reality is that many students know the basics but they don't understand how to apply it – and when we teach context separate to the text, they are still not able to do this. Rather than having a scattergun approach, I would reduce the context to two core aspects and then intertwine the key elements within them; for example, when teaching *Macbeth* I would condense context to:

- **Monarchy:** the role of a king; divine right and The Great Chain of Being; King James and the period 1603–1606, including the Gunpowder Plot; James's view of kingship and the *Basilikon Doron*[18]; the link between king and kingdom.

- **Gender:** societal expectations of gender; the role of women within marriages; the expectations of childbearing and maternal aspects of women; femininity and masculinity and how this affects physiology in women – for example, the belief that they were more physically affected by the emotions and the humours, and attitudes towards older (especially spinster or childless) women, who were often linked to witchcraft.

---

18 The *Basilikon Doron*, or 'The King's Gift' as translated from Greek, is here referencing King James's gift to his son, Henry, and took the form of a substantial letter which outlines the duties of kings to God, his office and his general behaviour. Further information can be found here: https://www.bl.uk/collection-items/printed-edition-of-king-james-vi-and-is-basilikon-doron-or-the-kings-gift-1603.

By concentrating on two strands throughout the teaching of the play, the aspects of each concept begin to overlap and so the context is at the heart of the play and how we understand it, rather than a detached consideration. Practically, a lot of this will be unpicked in discussions, where the separate ideas become intentionally intertwined. So, a typical thread of unpicking monarchy in the classroom might include the following types of questions at these key moments in the play:

- **Act II, sc. ii:** Why might Macbeth think he has lost his connection with God? Why is it important to Macbeth that he is able to pray? Does it matter that Duncan has died? Who has Macbeth betrayed? What is Shakespeare saying here about the connection between king and God?

- **Act III, sc. i:** Why does Macbeth think his power is empty? What difference does it make that Banquo's children will be king, if Macbeth already has the crown? Why is Macbeth so focused on Fleance when he clearly isn't a threat? What is Shakespeare saying here about a monarch's obsession with lineage?

- **Act IV, sc. iii:** Why does Malcolm choose to test Macduff's loyalty? Is Macduff loyal to Malcolm or to Scotland, and why does this matter? Macbeth now has power, so does it really matter if people know about the crimes he has committed? How can we link the list of sins to Macbeth's behaviour in the play – and does it matter if Macbeth has sinned? What is Shakespeare saying here about the role of a king?

There may be a need to introduce terms like *divine right, natural order, Chain of Being* – but these are only there to give students the vocabulary to articulate their ideas. The reality is that they need to understand the context – for example, how religion links to monarchy – and then once they understand this, and need a term for it, it's time to provide it. If we bolt on the information at the beginning and then tell students to add context into their essays, they will do what we have done: bolt it on. But if we weave the context into the heart of the play and make it central to the key moments we discuss, so will students. They will struggle to talk about Macbeth's character arc without considering contemporaneous attitudes to kingship, and their essays will include these ideas naturally. If we teach with a thread of context, students will write with it too – and they will get to the intricacies of the play, rather than understanding it at a surface level.

Much like with the teaching of themes and motifs, it is by threading the context carefully through the stories that leads Laura's students to those higher grades.

Applying it to the classroom

+ Begin by unpicking any misconceptions about Shakespeare's world. There can be many assumptions about gender, power and religion which are prevalent before we even begin to teach his plays. Images, such as the one used by Chris Curtis, can provide an opportunity to discuss perspectives on gender, class and society. Equally, using some historical sources (such as the speech by Elizabeth I) can be a good way in which to address these. Clarify contextual points, especially around beliefs such as *women had no power*, or *everyone had the same religious beliefs* or *there was no ethnic diversity in England during the period Shakespeare was writing*. These assumptions will potentially shape how students go on to read and interpret the plays.

+ Front-load some information about context but continue to weave it throughout the study of the play, relevant to the theme or character you are exploring. Too much decontextualised information about history not only risks us teaching a very different subject, but will also lead to paragraphs about context as opposed to students exploring how the writing may reflect the world it was written in. Whatever we notice about context needs to be rooted firmly in the text.

+ Consider how context may have impacted on performance. For example, the Globe was not only open-air but also very wedded to the idea of shared light (the same light between audience and performers, as opposed to artificial lighting), so artificial light would not have been used in that context. However, Blackfriars and other theatres may have made use of different lighting effects. Shakespeare's writing seems to favour the shared lighting of the Globe, but some of his later plays were likely to have been performed inside and lit by candles. This even has a potential impact on where breaks fall into the plays, as pauses were needed to trim the candles.

+ The Globe Theatre has an excellent virtual tour which is free to use and illustrates different elements of the staging with video examples.[19] This can be a perfect way to explore not only context but performance too – and could support students who have English as an additional language (EAL), as well as others; better still if you can give your students the experience of being in the Globe and imagining how that may have felt from the perspective of different audience members.

---

19 See https://www.shakespearesglobe.com/discover/about-us/virtual-tour/.

Chapter 2

Bringing Forth His Characters

Archetypes and people

One man in his time plays many parts

(*AYL*, II, vii, 142)

The study of character in literary texts, or *characterology*, has become a popular focus for our study of literature. This is closely linked to a psychological analysis of the text, with statements such as 'Hamlet was depressed', and 'Macbeth was suffering from post-traumatic stress' arising from this focus. That is not to say there are issues with this approach, but it is useful to be aware of where this stems from and where this may take us – particularly as we tend to then begin to unpick the motivations of the character, focusing on them as a realistic representation of an individual as opposed to a device. Shakespeare's use of soliloquy has certainly added weight to readings that focus on the emotions and psychology of the character, with this device used to reveal the interiority of some of his most significant characters, especially in his tragedies. This is a device used primarily in tragedies and histories, with the internal workings of tragic heroes or villains laid bare for all to see and hear.

Why teach it?

This is one of the areas students perhaps find most difficult when dealing with drama as opposed to realist fiction; understanding characters as devices rather than well-developed and autonomous individuals. Whilst this is true, novelists employ characters as devices too in drama, especially in drama that draws on the specific theatrical tradition of the mystery play – archetypal characters, used for their familiarity to the audience as much as for their specific traits, help to shape the performance, even where performers subvert the characteristics, aiming to challenge audience expectations.[1] Looking at characters like this is something of a threshold concept for our students; these are those points of comprehension where, if understood, the idea will change their thinking significantly. It is the threshold to a new understanding or way of thinking. This is much like the point where they begin to see the artist behind the art and stop seeing the text as a stream of consciousness or a self-actuating construct, sprung forth with barely a nod to audience and writer. If we can successfully enable students to see how characters are self-consciously constructed, with an awareness of readership and audience and an understanding of how they will relate to certain tropes, students will be more successful in considering not only the plays of Shakespeare, but other texts which they will examine.

What is it?

The more you learn about the plays and characters of Shakespeare, the more you become aware of certain recurring ideas, and this is most certainly true of his characters. The king, the daughter, the wife, the fool, the twins (fraternal or otherwise) and the soldier all appear across the body of his work and will have had certain resonance to his audience. As you will see later, his use of characters and ideas from classical and folk stories will have prompted his reader to understand these characters. The same characters even appear directly across his plays, with Falstaff, the fool and companion to Prince Hal in *1 Henry IV* and *2 Henry IV* and *The Merry Wives of Windsor*, unceremoniously removed from court by the now King Henry. He is also eulogised in *Henry V*. This recurring character is an interesting one and analysed extensively by Harold Bloom in *Falstaff: Give Me Life*.[2]

The king, the father and the blocker

The patriarchal figure is a powerful one, dominating many of Shakespeare's stories. From dead fathers in *Hamlet*, *Twelfth Night* and *Much Ado About Nothing*, to elderly and misguided ones in *King Lear*

---

1   Mystery plays are one of the earliest forms of drama in Europe, developed in the medieval period. These told the stories of the Bible, often in tableaux, and aimed to recreate key moments (such as Adam and Eve in Eden) and would often be performed for days in churches.

2   Harold Bloom, *Falstaff: Give Me Life* (New York: Scribner, 2017).

and *The Tempest*, they often dominate the tales. Kings, of course, provide a key focus for the history plays and often cross over in the role of the father too. Lady Macbeth, on preparing to kill King Duncan, claims she would have killed the old man himself 'had he not resembled my father' (*Macb.*, II, i, 14–15). The kingship of Duncan, and indeed the concept of kingship more widely, is an interesting area to explore in *Macbeth*. Duncan is associated with an aged wisdom: kind, innocent and firmly linked to an understanding of divine right and The Great Chain of Being, an idea the then monarch, James, had been keen to promote in his *Divinity of Kings* tome.[3] However, like Lear, Duncan also displays a naivety and lack of foresight that ultimately leads to his demise. Just as Lear is unable to see the danger before him in the form of his daughters – greedy for power and cruel in their methods – so is Duncan unable to see his own downfall in the guise of Macbeth. He trusts too quickly and fails to guard against the threats that surround him. He has already experienced the treachery of Cawdor and yet he continues to expose himself to peril, seemingly having learned nothing from these past experiences. This is something which Macbeth is determined to avoid, killing all those who may threaten his position, and Malcolm demonstrates another form of kingship, prepared to use whatever may be at his disposal to regain control of Scotland.

Other kings and leaders in the histories present perhaps a more positive view of leadership, with Henry's ascent to the throne seeing him throw off childish things, in the form of Falstaff, and adopting a more humble and inclusive leadership in which he says:

> I am not covetous for gold,
> Nor care I who doth feed upon my cost;
> It yearns me not if men my garments wear;
> Such outward things dwell not in my desires

> (*Hen. V*, IV, iii, 24–27)

This is rather different to the grasping, ambitious kings who stalk the stage in some of the other famous plays.

However, the concerns around weak, unethical leadership continue to pervade the plays, as does the notion of the burden of leadership.

---

3   Matthew Willis, 'Making Sense of the Divine Right of Kings', *JSTOR Daily* (18 December 2020). Available at: https://daily.jstor.org/making-sense-of-the-divine-right-of-kings/.

Shakespeare's father figures, many of whom are leaders in society too, often perform the function of the *blocker* – a familiar role in traditional narratives. They are there to be overcome; a barrier to true happiness. *A Midsummer Night's Dream*, *The Taming of the Shrew*, *A Winter's Tale*, *The Tempest* and *Romeo and Juliet* all include fathers who are, depending on your viewpoint, protecting their daughters from the dangers of the world outside, but equally preventing them from their pursuit of true happiness. Ophelia becomes a political pawn in Polonius's political games and in *Pericles* we reveal a father who is sleeping with his own daughter. They are figures of authority, often representing society – much as with family as a whole – and are often controlling and manipulative. They isolate their daughters from the rest of the world and would frequently rather see the death of their daughters rather than hear of their dishonour or disobedience. Hero in *Much Ado About Nothing*, Juliet in *Romeo and Juliet* and Cordelia in *King Lear* are all constrained by the whims of their fathers, indicative of ideas of property and gender.

Exploring the parent–child relationship with students can be a particularly useful way to begin examining the plays as it is something which, even with the best relationships, students can very much identify with.

The mother, the queen and the hag

Mothers are notoriously absent in many of Shakespeare's plays, with Lear's daughters – Ophelia, Desdemona and Hero – all notably motherless. In *Romeo and Juliet*, the deficit of Juliet's mother (seemingly distant from her daughter and unsympathetic to her pleas not to marry) is emphasised by her relationship with the Nurse, filled with a closeness and care absent in the actual mother–daughter relationship. Those who are there don't fare much better in Shakespeare: older women and those with questionable maternal instincts. In *Coriolanus*, his mother, Volumnia, seeks to maintain her own power within Rome through her political ambitions for her son. She is proud of his status as a heroic soldier, referring to his wounds as if medals of honour – 'He had, before this last expedition, twenty-five wounds upon him' – (*Coriol.*, II, i, 171–2) and persuading him to play out her own ambitions:

> let
> Thy mother rather feel thy pride than fear
> Thy dangerous stoutness, for I mock at death

With as big heart as thou. Do as thou list,
Thou valiantness was mine, thou suck'dst it from me

(*Coriol.*, III, ii, 125–129)

The parallels with Lady Macbeth are clear and Volumnia's techniques to persuade her son to her ends echo the words of Lady Macbeth who 'shame[s] to wear a heart so white' (*Macb.*, II, ii, 65–66). Both women seek greater powers for their 'partner in greatness' (*Macb.*, I, v, 14), but ultimately realise they are unable to control what it is they unleash. Coriolanus joins with his enemy in an attempt to sack Rome and Volumnia needs to beg him, along with his wife and son, to spare the city. His weakness is ultimately revealed to be her, and his agreement to spare the city leads to his destruction. Macbeth no longer needs his wife's counsel as his tyranny takes hold, leaving her wracked with guilt and her implied suicide. The 'fiend-like queen' (*Macb.*, V, vii, 98) we see in this play recurs in the mother figures Shakespeare deploys, much like the wicked queens of fairy tales. In *Pericles*, Dionyza tries to kill her adopted daughter; in *Cymbeline* the wicked queen/stepmother once again attempts to kill the stepchild and place her own son, Cloten, on the throne; and Gertrude in *Hamlet* is prepared to maintain her place on the throne by marrying her dead husband's brother. The question as to how much she was complicit in the murder is one which Hamlet and the audience must continue to puzzle. Lady Macbeth's barbarity, of course, seems to know no bounds as she talks with brutality about the murder of her imagined child – 'I would […] have pluck'd my nipple from his boneless gums, and dash'd his brains out, had I so sworn as you' (*Macb.*, I, vii, 57–8) – and calls on spirits to strip her of any semblance of femininity, or even humanity, in order to empower herself to go forth with her plan to kill the king. This stripping of her humanity and association with dark powers links her with the witches earlier in the play and the use of the older women in his plays to represent evil deeds and desires is perhaps indicative to societal attitudes towards older women during this period. No longer capable of childbearing, these women are either deleted from the plays, no longer serving the required function or cast as villains full of unnatural desires, hungry for power and prepared to go to any lengths to achieve this.

Mothers therefore in his plays are either absent or dysfunctional, with even Lady Capulet's presence seeming to emphasise the distance between her and her daughter. The alternatives are monstrous, and as Janet Adelman argues, *suffocating*.[4]

The soldier

The role of a soldier who returns from war is a complex one. Indeed, they fit into their new context and adopt a position unfamiliar to them, untrained and unacclimatised; something that continues to be a concern in the modern day. Returning soldiers are a recurrent concept in Shakespeare's plays, from *Much Ado About Nothing* to *Othello*. *Coriolanus* is perhaps the most extreme example, no longer regarding himself as a man, frequently referring to himself as a 'thing' throughout the play and more a weapon of war or machine than a man, scarred and moulded by his experiences on the battlefield. As he attempts to become 'author of himself' (*Coriol.*, V, iii, 36) – rewriting his position within his new world and, attempting, and failing, to resist the ambitions of his mother – he is renamed and redefined, but ultimately lost in this new world he needs to navigate. Equally, Macbeth's tactics on the battlefield do not translate well into his position as king, and tyranny and bloodshed become the signature of all he does once he is no longer a soldier.

The fool

The character of the fool predates Shakespeare and, were you to examine the history of madness, you would see that *idiots* and *madmen* are a significant part of the world which would have led to their appearance on his stage. There are also the court jesters, in the form of Feste from *Twelfth Night*, Trinculo in *The Tempest* and the clown in *Othello* and *Titus Andronicus*, but the character (or a reference to them) appears in 27 of his 37 plays.

Fools often do not play by the same rules as their *masters* or those around them and are often outside of some of the usual bounds of social order, with Feste moving between the houses of the two different households in *Twelfth Night* with apparent ease. They bring elements of the carnivalesque to the plays, often capering and contorting alongside their

---

4   Janet Adelman, *Suffocating Mothers: Fantasies of Maternal Origin in Shakespeare's Plays, Hamlet to The Tempest* (London: Psychology Press, 1992).

songs and witticisms, provoking some much-needed comic relief.[5] They also seem to have a freedom to speak in ways which would not be accepted from characters of a different position; for example, the truth that the Fool in *King Lear* offers to the King is at times sharp and brutal, offering Lear his 'coxcomb' in exchange for the crown, calling him out for the fool he is. The fool often speaks more truth than those characters around him, either wrapped up in riddles and songs (as with Feste and double plays), or in the words of the Porter in *Macbeth*, dark in their presence. The idea of the fool that sees again predates Shakespeare, as does the supposed wise man who is blind. In *King Lear*, neither the King nor the supposedly wise Gloucester can see the truth and it is only when they are blinded, either by their madness or the vicious attack from Lear's daughter, Goneril, they can begin to see the truth of the world around them.

In classical literature we have the character of Cassandra, the priestess of Apollo, cursed to speak the truth but dismissed as a madwoman. We also have Tiresias, who is given the gift of foresight but cursed by blindness after seeing Athena bathing. Both are dismissed by others, but both have understanding beyond that of the main protagonists. With characters such as these foregrounding his work, to dismiss Shakespeare's fools as simple comedic interludes would be a mistake. They certainly often bring laughter, as the likes of Touchstone or Feste caper across the stage, but they equally offer truth and wisdom to a degree beyond others and are often ignored in their wisdom. However, when you look to them, the message is clear to the audience and the reader: ignore these characters at your peril. Tracing their words with students can bring new insights, not only into Shakespeare's intentions, but into the errors of his main protagonists. How many are too proud to listen to the words of their fools or the blindmen who seek to warn them? How many are made fools by their lack of insight?

---

5   Mikhail Bakhtin, *Rabelais and His World*, tr. Helene Iswolsky (Bloomington, IN: Indiana University Press, 2009). Mikhail Bakhtin explored the ideas of the carnivalesque and grotesque in medieval literature and culture and examined how the inversion of social hierarchies were a key part of European culture, especially in relation to the lower classes.

How to teach it

Some of these characters will be familiar to your students already as they fall within the character and narrative structures that form much of our storytelling, drawing on the features identified by the likes of Propp and Todorov.[6] The troubled king, the wicked king, the hero/solider and the fool or madman will have been a feature of stories they will have encountered; *The Lion King*[7] mirrors the plot of Hamlet, for example, or the story of *Snow White* with the wicked stepmother and the heroes. Building on this familiarity once again can be a useful starting point, providing a way for students to already feel they understand how these characters function. What Shakespeare often provides us with is an opportunity to explore the motivations and inner complexity of these characters through his language.

Tracing character development is always a satisfying process – for example exploring how Lear descends into total madness, if he indeed was not mad to begin with, or seeing how the relationship between Macbeth and Lady Macbeth erodes over the course of the play. Again, this is a very characterological approach, so reminding students to return to the function or role of the character is just as important as the psychological dissection they will inevitably undergo. It is essential, then, to explore these alongside a range of fiction, especially those stories which do not only present a naturalistic approach, but are allegorical. Again, this is where fairy tales and myths can provide a useful vehicle for the discussion around the role of the character, fitting them into Propp and Todorov's theories of narratives, or Joseph Campbell's ideas around archetypes in his seminal work around the hero's journey.[8] Equally, though, by exploring texts such as Orwell's *Animal Farm* or Priestley's *An Inspector Calls*, where characters are clearly used as vehicles for ideas as opposed to fully formed, naturalistic individuals, we can begin to discern the messages within a text and the concepts which we will be able to explore throughout literature.

In this case study from Haili Hughes, an author, English teacher and the head of education at Iris Connect, she explains how she developed an

---

6   Vladimir Propp, *Morphology of the Folk Tale*, tr. Laurence Scott (Bloomington, IN: The American Folklore Society and Indiana University, 1968); Tzvetan Todorov, *The Fantastic: A Structural Approach to a Literary Genre*, tr. Richard Howard (New York: Cornell University Press, 1975).
7   *The Lion King*, dir. Roger Allers and Rob Minkoff [film] (Disney, 1994).
8   Joseph Campbell, *The Hero with a Thousand Faces*, 3rd edn (Novato, CA: New World Library, 2012).

approach to teaching the character of Lady Macbeth by focusing on a psychoanalytic critical lens, concentrating on the role of the character without losing sight of how we can connect students to their learning.

What might Freud say? How using critical theory transformed my teaching of Macbeth through a university lecture-style approach

I trained to teach in the late 2000s, and discovery learning was the overriding approach in our university sessions. I have memories of workshops on de Bono's thinking hats, where my course leader brought out baskets of different hats for us to wear, demonstrating how they could be used as a lesson prop to encourage students to think about texts in different ways. We learnt about differentiation through visual, auditory and kinaesthetic learning – how we could formulate questionnaires for students to fill in and then tailor our tasks during the lesson to the three different learning styles. At this point also, social media was just taking off and when we weren't spending sessions learning how to teach war poetry by turning the tables and chairs into trenches in our classrooms, we were getting to grips with how we could get students to make Facebook profiles for key characters in texts, to encourage students to consider what they may be thinking or feeling. It was all great fun and I looked forward to completing my PGCE so that I could put some of these strategies into practice.

But after a decade or so, I started to feel frustrated. The students just didn't seem to be thinking critically enough. They didn't write like scholars or seem to have the depth of knowledge required to achieve the top grades. Whilst on maternity leave, I started to read educational research. This was only just being encouraged in my school and I felt like the eight years between me completing a master's in teaching and learning and where I found myself then were a bit of a pedagogical wasteland; I had been doing what I had always done before and not adapted, as I wasn't sure how to. Educational research hadn't really been mentioned on my PGCE course at all, it seemed – and I was interested in finding out how pupils learnt and how I could maximise my lesson time, so I applied to study a master's in psychology to develop my knowledge. That's when my professional life completely changed, with the discovery of a paper by Kirschner, Sweller and Clark which explained the differences between experts and novices and stated that minimally guided instructional approaches are less effective and efficient than instructional approaches which give more guidance and scaffolding.[9] This blew my mind as it flew in the face of everything I had been taught and always done around the more constructivist, problem-based, discovery learning approach.

So began my journey of self-discovery – from Sweller to Barak Rosenshine.[10] I vowed that when I returned to school, I would completely change my approach and explore whether it yielded better results. The Education Endowment Foundation's *Metacognition and Self-regulated Learning*[11] recommendations also came at exactly the right time. I had an amazing top set who I had taught since Year 7 and had already laid some really great groundwork with in Year 10. In an attempt to challenge them appropriately, I had taught them different texts from the rest of the year group, opting for *Great Expectations* rather than *A Christmas Carol* as I wanted them to get to grips with a hefty text choice prior to higher education. When reflecting on my own experience of doing an English literature A level and degree, I had been shocked to feel the difference between GCSE and higher study. I was suddenly expected to read really complex journal articles and critical theory and I didn't feel like the course at GCSE had prepared me at all. I also began to reflect on how dry the GCSE course now seemed. Although more rigorous post-2015, like many English teachers, I had noticed fewer students were choosing to study English in further and higher education than had previously, and this both worried and upset me. I felt like I had not only a moral responsibility to facilitate the best grades possible for these students but to also imbue

---

9   Paul Kirschner, John Sweller and Richard E. Clark, 'Why Minimal Instruction Doesn't Work', *Educational Psychologist* 41(2) (2006): 75–86. Available at: http://dx.doi.org/10.1207/s15326985ep4102_1.

10 Barak Rosenshine, 'Principles of Instruction: Research-Based Strategies That All Teachers Should Know', *American Educator* 36 (2012): 12–39. Rosenshine explores the ways in which effective instructors use key elements such as: introducing new material in small steps; daily, weekly and termly review; and modelling. In this paper he identifies ten different principles that are effective tools for teaching – and in the teaching of Shakespeare, with its additional levels of complexity, these can be a useful way to approach the topic.

11 Education Endowment Foundation, *Metacognition and Self-Regulated Learning* (27 April 2017). Available at https://educationendowmentfoundation.org.uk/education-evidence/guidance-reports/metacognition.

a love of my subject. I recalled that reading academic criticism had really lit a flame for me, igniting a passion for literature – and the excitement of seeing a text through a different lens or perspective seemed like a great strategy to make literature more tantalising to students, as well as preparing them for further study.

It started off with Journal Fridays: we would spend an hour of our two-hour double using reciprocal reading strategies, with each table reading and attempting to decipher and make sense of an article related to what we had been learning in one of our literature texts that week. They would then spend the next hour working on embedding some of those ideas into an essay or exam response seamlessly, using them to try and formulate a more conceptualised response.

One of the lenses my class enjoyed the most was a psychoanalytical one – particularly looking at the work of Sigmund Freud in relation to Lady Macbeth. Some of the students had already heard about Freud in other lessons or had heard reference to him on a Netflix mystery programme about serial killers![12] So, this grabbed their attention straight away. The groundwork had already been laid about what critical lenses were, using an excellent resource I found being shared on Twitter where the different theoretical approaches had been explained using glasses frames, so I started by expounding a bit more on how psychoanalysis deals with the processes of understanding why people behave the way they do and what is going on in their subconscious to influence their choices.[13] After an introduction to Freud himself and his concept of id, ego and superego, we began to explore how these ideas might relate to Lady Macbeth. The students found quotations that linked to Lady Macbeth's overbearing id characteristics and how her superego is almost non-existent. We discussed the idea that Lady Macbeth may be suffering from a psychological disorder through some dialogic teaching activities, where students had to reason, discuss, argue and explain their point of view on this statement.

They were also fascinated by the whole concept of the Oedipus and Electra complex. They loved the idea of Lady Macbeth being jealous

---

12 *Freud*, dir. Marvin Kren [TV series] (Netflix, 2020).
13 For further resources, see: https://www.tes.com/teaching-resource/literary-criticism-a-level-feminism-marxism-psychoanalysis-queer-theory-etc-11581782.

of masculine power and how she offers to leave behind her femininity, craving the kind of power she can only achieve by being male. They loved the idea that the murder of Duncan was almost like a parricide, as he would have been regarded as the father of Scotland – a link to further explore with Oedipus, as Macbeth says after the murder, 'What hands are here! Ha! they pluck out mine eyes' (*Macb.*, II, ii, 60) just like Oedipus plucked out his after killing his own father.

A particularly compelling point which students kept returning to from Freud is the concept of childlessness as a punishment. The barrenness of Lady Macbeth and Macbeth in the play can be seen as a huge catalyst for their actions and students enjoyed considering the idea that her psychosis could be a result of losing so many children in infancy and the feelings of impotence she may have experienced at not fulfilling this role expected of her in society. They also discussed the idea that perhaps Lady Macbeth's feelings of frustration and ridiculing of his manhood comes from this inability to give her a child and he would do anything to seem more masculine to her, his desires to be a powerful king proving his manhood.

Crucially, I didn't want critical theory to just be an add-on. It was vital that pupils were able to embed the theoretical ideas into their own analysis, which is why I always made links explicit by signposting scenes they could re-annotate through this lens or encouraging them to link the new perspectives to particular bits of context we had learnt. Once the university-lecture-style direct instruction of the theory had been explained by me, we would then reread and annotate a scene and watch me writing a model paragraph on the visualiser, where I would explain how I had embedded the theory into an analytical response. The students were then ready to try some independent practice themselves, focusing on using the ideas as a springboard for their own response. I am not sure whether it was just this approach, but on results day I was astonished and thrilled to see that the class achieved 12 grade 9s and no fewer than 18 of them went on to study English at A level, with one about to leave to study English literature at Cambridge in September. It's even led to us embedding some critical theory at Key Stage 3 and re-energised our approach as a department.

Applying it to the classroom

+ Teach about archetypes and narrative structures so students can understand their role in the plays. Understanding the key components to villains, heroes and anti-heroes will allow students to examine the conventions and how Shakespeare utilises and subverts expectations.

+ Spend time considering the role of different characters and make explicit the distinction between them as characters in the realist tradition. Looking at morality and mystery plays can be useful here, as can looking at other allegories, including fairy tales. They can form a useful basis for thinking about the different roles characters fulfil and what they might represent in the texts. When teaching about the idea of heroes and villains I often drew on students' knowledge of popular culture as a starting point for our discussions around the play. Machiavellian characters, such as Scar in *The Lion King*, can shed new light when looking at the role of Iago in *Othello*.

+ Get students to trace the language Shakespeare is associating with the characters; for example, how the word brave is used in relation to Macbeth, casting him initially as a hero to later be replaced with tyrant – a word associated with villainy. What impact does that have on the audience? This is an interesting thread to explore in relation to the character of Snape in the *Harry Potter* books, as our feelings towards him shift and change across the series.

+ Make comparisons between characters and across different plays to understand how Shakespeare uses these devices more widely and to consider how he exploits differences. Some schools devote time at Key Stage 3 to analysing villains, heroes or familial relationships in a range of plays, as well as looking at a whole play so students have a firm grasp of the role these characters play as devices.

+ Trace the development (or lack of development) of characters. What is Shakespeare aiming to address here? Consider how they are introduced to the play. Entrances and exits are an important element of drama and often there is a delay in meeting the main protagonist and they are introduced by other means. For example, we learn about Macbeth from two different sources before he arrives on the stage: first via the witches and then in the reports from the battlefield. Immediately we have a sense of duality in terms of who he actually is; the man who will meet the witches or the hero of the battlefield, or something else? The opening lines of key characters are also important places to focus as we consider what it revealed about them there.

Chapter 3

Bringing Forth His Allusions

The Bible, the Classics and the Stories of Common Folk

I am here with thee and thy goats, as the most capricious poet, honest

Ovid, was among the Goths.

Touchstone (*AYL*, III, iii, 8–9)

Why teach it?

Shakespeare is one of the most consciously crafting writers we may encounter in our school lives and his source material's reimaginings of old stories and classical and biblical allusions are a key part of his work. As I explore in Chapter 1, the world of Shakespeare was not a world of homogenous Elizabethans and Jacobites. Much is often made about their relationship with religion and the reign of Henry, and his daughter, had indeed made this an interesting time in terms of the Church and religion. Elizabeth herself ensured all readily available copies of the Bible in the English language were Protestant ones and the arrival of James in 1603 came with its own set of challenges. However, it is hugely simplistic to make statements, such as I often see in essays about Shakespeare, that everyone in his time was really religious and that is why he makes so many references to the Bible.

Teaching students the specifics of these types of allusion in Shakespeare's work can be an important way for them to obtain a greater understanding of his ideas and his relationship with his audience and to consider his intentions. There are still many students who don't believe writers really try to engage with their reader when they are producing their work. They hang onto the idea of writing as a personal act of expression. Even the prevalent view that Shakespeare was predominantly a performer and didn't care much about publishing is now being contested, with emerging evidence that he was consciously aware of what his readership might be interested in and considered the power his allusions may have on them.

What is it?

Shakespeare's sources are wide and showed quite how learned he was. These included the plays and poems of other writers which were often reworked, commonplace amongst writers of this period, and historical sources such as *Holinshed's Chronicles* providing source material for more than a third of his plays.[1] This was also the source material for many of Shakespeare's contemporaries, including Marlowe and Spenser.

Shakespeare, like his contemporaries, was grammar-educated and his studies of classics as well as plays of the period were influential to his writing. The plot of *The Comedy of Errors* was inspired by Plautus' comedy *Menaechmi*, considered a staple of grammar school education and is a story Shakespeare and his contemporaries would have been familiar with. For his Roman plays, Shakespeare took his inspiration from Sir Thomas North's translation of Plutarch's *Lives of the Noble Grecians and Romans* and he famously drew the plots for *Romeo and Juliet* and *Much Ado About Nothing* from the work of Italian writer Giovanni Boccaccio.

However, not all of his influences are obvious – and allusions to the Bible, classical stories and myths of Greece, based in part on the work of Ovid, and folktales would have been more familiar to some of his readers and audience than they are perhaps to us now. They formed part of an intellectual exercise for the writer and the audience. To clarify, an allusion is an expression we use that is designed to call something to mind without mentioning it explicitly. It is an indirect or passing reference to which we will evoke associations with other stories or ideas the writer wants to incorporate. For example, we may allude to stories we know people will be familiar with across our culture, talking about

---

1   See https://www.bl.uk/collection-items/holinsheds-chronicles-1577.

winners of golden tickets with a nod to Roald Dahl's *Charlie and the Chocolate Factory* for those who have had a lucky find, or calling up images of Superman's Achilles' heel (another allusion) when we say that something is their kryptonite.

Biblical allusion

There has also been much speculation about Shakespeare's own religious views – and whilst it would have been likely his parents were Catholic, there are few definitives we can work from. However, what is certain is that allusions to the Bible come rapidly throughout, some undoubtedly because they had woven their way into the fabric of the minds of both the audience and the writer, much as we see today, without much consideration of the origin. Yet, the prevalence of a range of references does seem to suggest that Shakespeare, a man conscious of his choices of words and their relationship to both his audience and reader, has an engagement with the Bible that goes well beyond a passing knowledge. He, of course, does not only make reference to the Bible in his works. His use of classical allusion and references to history, folklore and stories of a pastoral idyll, as in *King Lear* and *Hamlet*, are abundant (see page 64). Hamlet was in part inspired by the story of Amleth, the Icelandic trickster figure, immortalised in the 13th century work of the historian Saxo Grammaticus in the third and fourth books of his *Gesta Danorum* (Story of the Danes),[2] once again suggesting links to stories predating Christianity and evoking a pagan world. However, biblical allusions, especially to the Old Testament, are to be found aplenty throughout the texts and, when approaching a play, having access to some of the most prevalent ones across his work can enrich and enliven a reading.

Genesis, the angels and Satan

Allusions to the story of Adam and Eve are prevalent throughout Shakespeare's work. In *Macbeth* we see reference to how Lady Macbeth urges her husband to hide his secret desires for kingship by looking 'the innocent flower' whilst hiding the 'serpent under it' (*Macb.*, I, v, 66–67) and in *Henry V* Canterbury talks of 'offending Adam out of him, leaving his body as a paradise' (*Hen. V*, I, i, 29–30). In the same passage from *Henry V*, it is the angel who 'whips' Adam from him, and references to

---

2   Saxo Grammaticus, *The Danish History, Books I–IX* [ebook] (Project Gutenberg, 2006 [1905]). Available at: https://www.gutenberg.org/files/1150/1150-h/1150-h.htm.

angels come again in *Macbeth* where they will 'plead trumpet-tongu'd' at the taking off of Duncan (*Macb.*, I, vii, 19). This is an allusion to both Matthew 24:31 and Revelations 8:2, 8:6, 8:13 and 9:14 where trumpeted angels will herald the arrival of the apocalypse, foreshadowing later events in the play where indeed Macbeth's world will end. Lady Macbeth also questions which 'hideous trumpet' wakes the sleepers in her house as the alarm rings to alert them of the murder (*Macb.*, II, iii, 89). Adam appears again in *The Comedy of Errors* with Dromio stating:

Not that Adam that kept the Paradise but that Adam

that keeps the prison: he that goes in the calf's

skin that was killed for the Prodigal; he that came

behind you, sir, like an evil angel, and bid you

forsake your liberty.

(*Com. Err.*, IV, iii, 16–20)

The allusions here are coming thick and fast as he references both the Prodigal son from Luke 15:11–32 and the evil angel. The evil angel, Satan, Lucifer or Beelzebub are directly referenced 19 times across his plays and the Devil or devils are referenced numerous times throughout his work, frequently as an insult. The allusions to Beelzebub in the Porter's scene in *Macbeth* (II, iii, 1–24) come in a speech often largely ignored in productions or focused on for its comic relief, but the passage itself is highly apocryphal, with the 'hell-gate' creating a link to Matthew 16:18 in which Christ says, 'And I say also unto thee, That thou art Peter, and upon this rock I will build my church; and the gates of hell shall not prevail against it.' This both links back to Macbeth's previous line where his killing of Duncan will 'summon' Duncan to 'heaven or to hell' (II, i, 64) and prepares us again to enter the apocalyptic scene Lennox will describe when he enters the castle (II, iii, 60–69). More recent productions have emphasised the role of the Porter as 'the fool who sees', with the 2018 Royal Shakespeare Company's production keeping him on stage, tallying the murders as they stack up and waiting for the final fall of Macbeth.[3]

The fall is also a significant theme in the plays, relevant to classical stories as well as the Bible. But *Macbeth* directly references the fall of Satan, with Malcolm warning MacDuff 'Angels are bright still, though the

---

3   *Macbeth*, dir. Polly Findlay (Royal Shakespeare Company, Royal Shakespeare Theatre, Stratford-upon-Avon, 2018).

brightest fell' (IV, iii, 22) as they discuss Macbeth's treachery. His jealousy of Duncan's sons certainly mirrors the actions of Satan in his
rebellion against God, as seen to be depicted later in Milton's *Paradise
Lost*.[4] In *Henry VIII*, Cardinal Worsley says he is beset by the same fate
as Lucifer, his 'high-blown pride' (*Hen. VIII*, III, ii, 362) leading him to
fall 'like Lucifer' (III, ii, 372). The sin of pride and ambition are sins of
biblical proportions.

Not all of Shakespeare's allusions to the heavens are of fallen angels,
however. Juliet is referred to as a 'bright angel' in the famous balcony
scene (*Rom. & Jul.*, II, ii, 26) and this is a concept which Baz Luhrmann
makes much of in his costume choices for Juliet in his cinematic production of the play; she is either shrouded in white or adorned with wings
to leave us in no doubt.[5] References to angels make frequent appearance
in both comedies and tragedies alike, either heralding heavenly wonders,
warring while men strive for good or ringing out the warnings to the
heavens.

Classical allusions

Shakespeare, it seems, was not only well versed in the world of the Bible
but in classical stories too. The website No Sweat Shakespeare suggests
there are '53 classical allusions in *Titus Andronicus*, 39 in *Antony and
Cleopatra*, 38 in *Love's Labour's Lost*, 37 in *A Midsummer Night's Dream*,
31 in *Cymberline*, 26 in *Coriolanus*, 25 in *Romeo and Juliet*, 25 in *All's
Well that Ends Well*, 25 in *Pericles*, 19 in *Hamlet*, 11 in *Othello*, 8 in
Macbeth and 8 in *King Lear*.'[6] Just as there is no doubt that Shakespeare
was knowledgeable in religious studies, there is no doubt that his education had led him to have a good understanding of some of these
well-known stories and characters. His relationship with Ovid is particularly significant and there are numerous references to *Metamorphoses*
throughout his work. *Troilus and Cressida* is, of course, a play set during
the Trojan War – and George Chapman, a fellow playwright and sometimes collaborator of his, had written his own translation of Homer's
works. Shakespeare was therefore not alone in both taking his inspiration from, as well as making allusion to, classical stories, with his

---

4   John Milton, *Paradise Lost* (London: Penguin Classics, 2003).
5   *William Shakespeare's Romeo + Juliet*, dir. Baz Luhrmann [film] (Bazmark Films, 1996).
6   See https://nosweatshakespeare.com/blog/shakespeare-us-of-mythology/.

contemporaries such as Christopher Marlowe and Thomas Middleton exploring these, including them in their works.[7]

Magical creatures and characters also make frequent appearances and not only in terms of the fae of *A Midsummer Night's Dream*, but throughout the language Shakespeare uses. They are now so common-place that we perhaps barely even register them. Take this extract from *3 Henry VI*:

> I'll drown more sailors than the mermaid shall;
>
> I'll slay more gazers than the basilisk,
>
> I'll play the orator as well as Nestor,
>
> Deceive more slily than Ulysses could,
>
> And, like a Sinon, take another Troy.
>
> I can add colours to the chameleon,
>
> Change shapes with Proteus for advantages,
>
> And set the murd'rous Machiavel to school.

(*3 Hen. VI*, III, ii, 186–193)

Here we have the mermaid, the basilisk and the chameleon; creatures not only of these fantastic tales but also of the folkloric world. However, we also have a reference to Nestor, the Greek leader in Troy, Ulysses, the hero of Homer's *Odyssey*, and Sinon from Virgil's *Aeneid*. The inclusion of Proteus – the sea god Neptune's shepherd, with his ability to change shape – is also referenced in *3 Henry VI* and is the name of one of the heroes of *The Two Gentlemen of Verona*, his duplicitous nature betrayed by his name to the audience. We are expecting someone who will shift his form from the very start, much as we know Mercutio's mercurial nature is unlikely to end well. Eliciting responses from the audience before they had even had time to consider many of the implications certainly seemed like a key skill of Shakespeare. In *Much Ado About Nothing*, Benedict declares:

> I would not marry her, though she
>
> were endowed with all that Adam had left him before he

---

7   Donald Jellerson, 'Haunted History and the Birth of the Republic in Middleton's *Ghost of Lucrece*', *Criticism* 53(1) (2011): 53–82. Available at: https://www.jstor.org/stable/23131555?seq=1# metadata_info_tab_contents.

transgressed: she would have made Hercules have turned spit, yea,

and have cleft his club to make the fire too. Come, talk not of her; you

shall find her the infernal Ate in good apparel. I would to God some

scholar would conjure her

(Much Ado, II, i, 260–267)

Once again, we have reference to Adam and his expulsion from the Garden of Eden but also Hercules, demasculinised by being dressed in women's clothing by Omphale – while she took his, leaving him to her *women's work* – and to the goddess Ate, a deity of discord and vengeance. In just a few short lines we are given a strong sense of exactly how Benedict feels about the idea of marriage.

Ovid

I have given a separate section to focus briefly on Shakespeare's relationship with the writing of Ovid. As the British Library article on Ovid's *Metamorphoses* argues, Ovid is widely considered to be Shakespeare's favourite author, and his influence can be found not only in his use of stories and language, but also in his use of metre and form with *Venus and Adonis* and *The Rape of Lucruce* regarded as explicitly Ovidian works.[8] He is also the only classical author who is directly referenced by Shakespeare, appearing in name as Ovidius Naso in *Love's Labour's Lost* (IV, ii, 125).

Ovid also provided source material that Shakespeare drew directly upon, with the story of Pyramus and Thisbe providing inspiration for *Romeo and Juliet* and the play within a play in *A Midsummer Night's Dream*. The story of two doomed lovers infuses other plays, with reference to 'So pale did shine the moon on Pyramus / When he by night lay bathed in maiden blood' in *Titus Andronicus* (*Tit. A.*, II, iii, 231–232) and in *The Merchant of Venice* when Jessica and Lorenzo ponder on the fates of lovers in past stories (*Merch. V.*, V, i, 1–19). Doomed lovers and virginal sacrifices (Ophelia, Macbeth and his Queen and, for a brief and tempestuous moment, Hero and Claudio, for example) appear as a concern within Shakespeare's texts. Other references to Ovid, particularly

---

8   See https://www.bl.uk/collection-items/ovids-metamorphoses.

Metamorphoses, appear elsewhere in Shakespeare's work, with Prospero's speech at the end of *The Tempest* alluding to the words of Medea in Book 7 of the text: Medea calls on 'Ye Ayres and windes: ye Elves of hilles, of Brookes, of Woods alone / Of standing Lakes' whilst Prospero calls on 'Ye elves of hills, brooks, standing lakes, and groves' (*Temp.*, V, i, 33). Both are declaring their power over nature, but also both make later reference to darker powers to call up 'dead men from their graves', or wake 'sleepers' from the graves (*Temp.*, V, i, 49).[9]

Shakespeare and Ovid also share a number of key concerns, as do many other writers, around aspects of sexuality and gender, transformation and the role these myths play in our society.

Folktales and folklore

Three is most certainly the magic number and Shakespeare is well aware of this. Folk and fairy tales where the number three plays a central role are aplenty. *The Three Little Pigs*, *Three Billy Goats Gruff* and *Goldilocks and the Three Bears* are all familiar stories to us and their roots are woven throughout our history with the three Fates from classical mythology, the three weapons of Odin, Thor and Freya in Norse tales and the idea of the Trinity occurring in many different religious stories. The third child in folktales is often the wisest one, rewarded for their wisdom, courage and bravery and the pattern of three attempts at something, as in Rumpelstiltskin, are common as you trace their origins back from the work of the Brothers Grimm.[10] In *King Lear* we have a version of the *Cinderella* tale, with two wicked sisters and one kind and wise one who is ultimately disowned and abandoned, only to come good at the end. In *The Merchant of Venice* there are the three caskets that Portia's suitors must select from in order to win her hand. Bassanio forgoes the gold and silver caskets, choosing the lead one in order to succeed. This is something which Freud made much of in his essay entitled 'The Theme of the Three Caskets', concluding that the three metal containers symbolise three different versions of womanhood, just as the three daughters in *King Lear* do.[11]

---

9 See https://www.bbc.co.uk/teach/why-is-the-bard-so-poular-abroad/zhcjrj6.

10 Jacob and Wilhelm Grimm, *The Complete Fairy Tales of The Brothers Grimm* (Hertfordshire: Wordsworth Classics, 2009).

11 Sigmund Freud, 'The Theme of the Three Caskets'. In *The Standard Edition of the Complete Psychological Works of Sigmund Freud, Volume XII (1922–1913)* (London: The Hogarth Press and The Institute of Pyscho-Analysis, 1958). Available at: https://www.sas.upenn.edu/~cavitch/pdf-library/Freud_ThreeCaskets.pdf.

Shakespeare also draws on the significance of the number three with the witches in *Macbeth*, an unholy trinity and as much a biblical allusion as drawing on the power of three which exists in folktales. This is emphasised in their triple greeting: 'All hail Macbeth! Hail to thee, Thane of Glamis! / All hail Macbeth! Hail to thee, Thane of Cawdor! / All hail Macbeth, that shall be king hereafter!' (*Macb.*, I, iii, 48–50). This is an allusion to the common greeting in the New Testament, perhaps most poignantly to Matthew 26:49, where Judas prepares to betray Jesus to the Sanhedrin and Roman soldiers. As the soldiers approach, Judas calls 'hail master' before he delivers his fatal kiss. Had we, the audience, recognised that allusion, then the intended betrayal could not be clearer. The relationship between Christian and pagan stories enables Shakespeare to draw upon ideas which will resonate with the audience in many ways. The tripling continues in *Macbeth*; the Porter talks of the three things which alcohol provoke, the 'brindle cat' mewed three times, three apparitions appear to Macbeth and his 'tomorrow and tomorrow and tomorrow' soliloquy (*Macb.*, V, v, 17–28) as the King muses on the futility of life. Tracing the number three in the play is an interesting activity and, as students understand the symbolic significance of this, they can again return to the conscious crafting that will support them to consider those bigger ideas Shakespeare wished to convey, and how we might respond to them.

Cymbeline is another play which uses many folkloric elements. As with *King Lear*, it is set in ancient Britain and harks back to a time of pastoral idyll, although equally one beset by conflict and division as the Romans seek to control the land. We have the wicked Queen/stepmother, with the usurping son she wishes to place on the throne. Set in the Welsh hills, although devoid of the shepherds of *A Winter's Tale* and *As You Like It*, *Cymbeline* sees a yearning to a lost past which is also evoked in *Lear*.

As mentioned in Chapter 5, which discusses language, symbols and motifs (see page 99), pastoral images and the natural world are also a feature in Shakespeare's plays; in particular, folkloric knowledge of these elements. If we look at Ophelia's piteous final scene in *Hamlet*, we see her adorn the onlookers with flowers. These weeds are suggestive of her state of mind and what she has endured:

> There's rosemary, that's for remembrance; pray,
> love, remember: and there is pansies, that's for thoughts. […]

There's fennel for you, and columbines; there's rue for you; and here's

some for me; we may call it herb of grace o' Sundays. O, you must

wear your rue with a difference! There's a daisy; I would give you some violets, but they withered all when my father died.

(*Haml.*, IV, iv, 173–184)

Rosemary was known to have properties associated with the memory, something which is still much cited. The same is true of pansies, and the sadness – as Ophelia asks for her remembrance, having been abandoned by Hamlet – is palpable. Fennel had become associated with a lack of substance, its seeds used as an appetite suppressant by fasting pilgrims in the Middle Ages. Columbine was the flower representative of ingratitude and makes an appearance in *Love's Labour's Lost*. The meaning of rue remains with us, and the regret and sorrow we feel for Ophelia at this point is almost tangible. Columbine was also used at one time as an abortifacient to prompt miscarriage – perhaps indicative of the sexual relationship between Hamlet and Ophelia alluded to throughout the play – and was used medicinally in many other ways. The daisy is frequently linked to innocence; this again resonates as we watch Ophelia's inevitable demise.

Some of Shakespeare's plays are also set in the pastoral world. *A Midsummer Night's Dream* and *As You Like It* provide a liminal space for characters to explore the complex issues of society; a safe space where they can subvert and cavort through leafy glades, hidden in the shade of the trees as they unpick the thorniest aspects of gender and sexuality. The use of setting here, as well as in *King Lear* and *Cymbeline*, allows a sense of nostalgia as well as drawing on the magical aspects of a world which was quickly becoming demystified with the emerging ideas of the period. It is notable that Shakespeare sets none of his plays in London, where they were so often performed. In fact, he frequently avoids real settings except with his histories, instead opting for foreign lands, distant islands and mysterious woodlands. The shadowy fairy folk in *A Midsummer Night's Dream* both mirror and untangle the difficulties we encounter within our everyday realities and, in doing so, allow us to reflect on them, the stage transporting us to otherworldly places and faraway realms to achieve this. Once upon a time, many years ago, in a land far, far away …

How to teach it

Introducing students to some of Shakespeare's influences can be a powerful way to ensure they consider the writer behind the art. One of the things students can find most challenging is to move beyond the text and consider the conscious crafting of the writer – and introducing them to the stories and ideas which influenced him can help them to see his hand at work and apply the same ideas to other writers, including themselves. Not only will that bring obvious benefits when students are reading his work and writing about it for examination, but these are good stories in themselves, whose reach goes well beyond their simple influences. There is also a universality about them, much as is argued about the work of Shakespeare, and themes and characters take on new resonances in new contexts. Making time for some of these stories in our curriculum and considering where they may appear elsewhere within the school (for example, drawing on the biblical teaching in religious studies or examining the relationship between church and state in history) can ensure that students are able to engage in the characters and stories Shakespeare is utilising in a different way. Just as his contemporaries enjoyed spotting allusions, so will our students, so preparing them for this by front-loading some stories and encouraging them to consider what they may already know will provide a good opportunity for them to engage in that game. Just as we trace language and imagery across his works, tracing the allusions can also help to bring the text to life; giving students short, allusion-rich extracts, where they can see how they are being used, will empower them to continue this as you read on.

This section has only just begun to explore the use of allusion in Shakespeare's work. The table that follows offers some further opportunities to examine where he uses biblical allusion in his writing:

Allusion to:	In:
Genesis	*Macbeth*: Lady Macbeth cast in the role of Eve, with references to the serpent layering up the significance of her role as the temptress. In addition, the fall of man is prevalent in many plays, the high standing of the male characters representative of

Allusion to:	In:
	fallen angels, not least in *Macbeth*, *Cymbeline* and *Love's Labour's Lost*.
The Crucifixion	Again, in *Macbeth* there is a reference to Golgotha (*Macb.*, I, ii, 41); this not only indicates the horror of the scene Macbeth and Banquo were recreating with the slaughter in battle, likening it to the place where one of the most terrible atrocities took place, but also alludes to the fall which will be forthcoming in the play.
	Resurrection also appears in his plays, especially concerning women, in *A Winter's Tale*, Imogen in *Cymbeline* and Thaisa in *Pericles*.
	The idea of betrayal and forgiveness is prevalent in many plays, but in *Richard II*, Richard often compares himself to Christ, creating a conscious parallel for the audience.
The apocalypse/The Book of Revelation	References to the end of days come frequently in texts such as *Measure for Measure*, *King Lear*, *Macbeth* and *Antony and Cleopatra*. In the latter, there are a number of references to a fallen star, with Cleopatra talking of Antony's imminent death in apocryphal terms: 'O sun! / Burn the great sphere thou mov'st in; darkling stand / The varying star o' the world.' (*Ant. & Cl.*, IV, viii, 9–12)
	The emotional implications of her outcry are clear, but so is the significance of the consequences of their love affair on the world as a whole.
Heaven and Hell	References to Heaven in Shakespeare's work are too numerous to gain much from listing

Allusion to:	In:
	them – there are 33 in *Romeo and Juliet* alone. These are often in relation to Romeo to his Juliet, once again cementing the idea of her angelic appearance and significance in his world. However, there are also five separate references to Hell within this text, with over 200 references to 'hell' or 'hellish' throughout his works. By again asking students to identify the meaning here, considering the implications of the extremes, they will be able to have a clearer understanding of what Shakespeare intended to convey at these moments. When Hamlet says he will approach the ghost seen on the battlements at the start of *Hamlet* – 'If it assume my noble father's person, I'll speak to it, though hell itself should gape And bid me hold my peace' (*Haml.*, I, ii, 243–245) – students familiar with what hell gaping might indicate about the importance of his actions can only enrich their understanding of Hamlet's state of mind and how Shakespeare's audience may react to those who dabble with the supernatural.

Applying it to the classroom

+ Anticipate the stories and allusions that will come up in your curriculum later and pre-teach these. Not only do these have great value in themselves, but it will also mean students are already primed to understand their place in Shakespeare's work. Look too at alternative versions of the stories which he drew upon to think about the revisions he made and the implications of these.

+ Discuss how allusions and world-building are used outside of Shakespeare and how self-referential tropes are used throughout our film and popular culture. Superhero films, the world of *Harry Potter* and the work of Philip Pullman are good examples where references to classical stories and internal referencing are used frequently. Examine the effect this has on the audience before applying it to Shakespeare.

+ Trace allusions across a text and consider why Shakespeare might be employing them for his audience and reader. What might these tell us about a character or a theme? Discuss how an audience, aware of an allusion, may respond at that point. Once you have begun to make links to Richard's references to himself as Christ-like, is that ironic, suggestive of his hubris or does it draw our sympathies?

+ Consider how these allusions help to form patterns in his language and his concepts – for example, the ideas of angels, fallen stars and Lucifer. What clues may these hold to enrich our reading of his text?

+ Look at how allusions to Shakespeare now form part of our language. See how many students can spot when reading other works, or even in the news and day-to-day language we use.

Chapter 4

Bringing Forth His Themes

Leadership, Love, Gender and Conflict

A woman impudent and mannish grown,
Is not more loath'd than an effeminate man,

(Tr. & Cr., III, iii, 128–129)

Why teach it?

Just as with his characters and his language, Shakespeare returns to certain themes and ideas over and again in his plays. It is easy to assume that these were not just the concerns of the playwright but those of his readership and audience. These are themes which predate Shakespeare, of course, and ideas about power, gender and tensions between the state and the individual are all concerns we can see threaded throughout both Shakespeare's source material and the works of literature that followed. When we focus on the themes of the text, we are in a stronger position to elicit the conceptual thinking from our students that is needed. If they can begin to think about the big ideas and questions that the writer is grappling with, then they will be able to construct much clearer arguments around his writing and their response to this. This then allows them to explore what he may have wanted to say, how he was saying it and why it matters. This sits within a popular approach to essay writing, whereby students begin with a thesis statement where they identify *what* Shakespeare wanted to achieve – *Shakespeare presents Romeo as a man who is conflicted in his own masculinity, depicting a version of manhood which conflicts with the prevalent ideas of the society in which he was presented* – before they go on to examine the methods he deploys to do so, including language and stagecraft. This is a vehicle for much more effective exploration of the text, with *why* he wanted to do so woven through the essay, reflecting on the significance in terms of context and his audience.

What are they?

The themes Shakespeare explored are varied and each one would be worthy of a book in itself. However, this next section will attempt to summarise the most significant ideas around some of the most prevalent ones: love, power and leadership, conflict, romantic and mixed-gender relationships, the position of women during the Renaissance, gender and sexuality.

Love

Shakespeare is often known first and foremost as a purveyor of romantic love. His sonnets have become synonymous with romance and his two great doomed lovers, Romeo and Juliet, are often called upon when we wish to speak of great loves, or even fickle ones, dubbing those who are successful in their romantic escapades as *Romeos*. However, there is a great deal more nuance in his exploration of ideas of love and he concerned himself with it in many different forms:

+ Familial love, especially those between daughters and fathers, is a central theme. *Romeo and Juliet, A Midsummer Night's Dream, Much Ado About Nothing, The Tempest* and *King Lear* all centre upon the love, and indeed tensions, between these characters. In these plays the desires of the individual, either the parent or the child, provide a focus for the action, often aping the conflicts within society as a whole (see also the section on blockers on page 44 and the later section on gender in his plays on page 77).

+ Fraternal and platonic love provides a central theme to many of his plays too and Romeo's tensions are not only related to familial loyalty but to those of the love he had for his *brothers*. His relationship with Mercutio, and his subsequent desire for revenge, provides the final catalyst for the tragedy. Equally, the love between the men in *The Two Gentlemen of Verona, Othello* and *As You Like It* provides the central conflict of the plays. Emma Smith, in her lectures on the plays, argues that it is these brotherly bonds and ideas of loyalty that are most challenged in his writing – and the breaking of these, as romantic love and marriage come to the fore, is perhaps one of the most significant recurring themes.[1] Many critics have made much of the homoerotic overtones of this and speculation as to Shakespeare's own sexuality frequently circulates as a result, especially in relation to his sonnets to the 'fair youth' (see the section on queer studies on page 13. Sibling rivalry too is a recurring notion, with the brothers (and indeed sisters) in *King Lear* battling over who holds the power.

+ Romantic, unrequited and courtly love is, of course, perhaps the most discussed element of his writing. Wordsworth, in his poem 'Scorn not the Sonnet', reminds the critics they should pause in their mockery and remember that the sonnets were a 'key' with which 'Shakespeare unlocked his heart',[2] an idea echoed by Robert Browning in his poem 'House'.[3] A quick Google search will lead you to hundreds of quotes that would be suitable for anything from Valentine's Day to adding to wedding vows, and the film *Shakespeare in Love* continued to present him as a man filled with passions and desires as a very human version of the person behind the words.[4]

Power and leadership[5]

Power – who holds it and who wants it – is a key theme in Shakespeare's work. It pervades the discussions around gender, ethnicity and age, with children frequently battling with their parents, often to comedic effect, in order to take control. Shakespeare often focuses his attention on those in power: kings and queens and the patrician class. However, woven within this is the issue of class. It is easy to dismiss this as high drama, yet the interactions between these characters and those they rule provide a layer of conflict, highlighting the difficulties between those who hold power and those who don't. *Coriolanus* is a play that has been used by many to explore this exact point, with Bertolt Brecht adapting

---

1   Emma Smith, University of Oxford: *Approaching Shakespeare* [podcast], Episodes 1, 10 and 42 (2010–2017). Available at: https://podcasts.ox.ac.uk/series/approaching-shakespeare.
2   William Wordsworth, 'Scorn not the Sonnet'. Available at: https://rpo.library.utoronto.ca/content/scorn-not-sonnet.
3   Robert Browning, 'House'. In Bliss Carman (eds.), *The World's Best Poetry, Vol. VII: Descriptive Poems, Narrative Poems* (Philadelphia: John D. Morris & Co., 1904). Available at: https://www.bartleby.com/360/7/79.html.
4   *Shakespeare in Love*, dir. John Madden [film] (Miramax, 1998).
5   See also the section on kings and fathers on page 44.

it to fully exploit ideas of alienation and the tragedy of the workers as opposed to their leader. Coriolanus – a patrician by birth – is removed from his people, refusing to yield to them, unwilling to not 'play the man I am' (*Coriol.*, III, ii, 14–15).

Coriolanus is not the worst of the leaders Shakespeare presents, however (although deeply unlikable), with tyrants, murderers and monsters, in the form of Richard III, destroying their kingdoms in their pursuit of power, riddled with their own paranoia. 'O! full of scorpions is my mind' (*Macb.*, III, ii, 36) despairs Macbeth, unable to rest easy in his throne or his bed as he anticipates the next threat that awaits him. That is not to say that Shakespeare does not encourage sympathy for those who lead, such as Lear whose lack of wisdom and arrogance leads to not only the fragmentation of England, but of his own mind. Shakespeare knows leadership comes at a price, reminding us in 2 *Henry IV*, 'uneasy lies the head that wears the crown' (III, i, 31). There is a burden to leadership and a corrupting element to this from which those who seek it may not escape. Even Malvolio, prancing in his yellow stockings in his mistaken belief that he has finally moved beyond his station and declaring 'some have greatness thrust upon them' (*Twel. N*, II, v, 158), reminds us in his humiliation that power is not something deserving of all. The idea of deserving power and kingship comes very much to the fore in *Macbeth*, with King James's notion of the divinity of kings reflected in the trumpeting of angels and the fall of those who dare usurp the rightful king. This recurs throughout his plays, exploring divine right and drawing on classical stories of wayward heirs returning to claim their position on the throne. Equally, ideas of lineage – especially in relation to the head of state – emerge again and again in the writing. Hamlet, the obvious heir to the Danish throne when considered in terms of the English system, does not immediately succeed to the throne in Danish law and there are a number of reasons for this. Macbeth succeeds when Duncan's sons flee Scotland, fearful for their safety, but spends the rest of the play considering his 'barren sceptre' and 'fruitless crown', that are indicative of the end of his line and his fragile grasp on power (*Macb.*, III, i, 61–62). This would be particularly apt at a time when James's own position as monarch came as a result of a supposedly virgin queen and the end of the Tudor reign.

Conflict: the individual and society

It is not only mistaken identity that is a central conceit in the plays, but also a constant return to the question of who we are and how we know that. Social status and identity in relation to this is often explored, with some characters having many different monikers. Others are defined simply by their role, as with the Duke in *Measure for Measure*. In plays such as *The Comedy of Errors* mistaken identity seems purely to be a comedic trope, but the doubling of names and the final reveal of who the characters are removes the previous fluidity of identity and provides security based upon how society can now define them. In addition, physical appearance – where simply adding a pair of trousers and a hat can not only change our status, but our gender and how we are perceived – is a recurring idea in the plays, often to much hilarity.

Comedic doubling and mistaken identity are deployed in *Twelfth Night*, examining not only issues of individual identity but gender and class too, as Viola finds herself in the position of a serving man, but there are also parallel plots and relationships in plays such as *A Midsummer Night's Dream* and *As You Like It*. The characters within these relationships can be seen as interchangeable, with *A Midsummer Night's Dream* seeming to suggest nothing short of a partner-swapping farce. Within the confines of magical forests, islands and indeed, plays, who is who, who loves who and, quite often, where they are, creates a cacophony of chaos which entertains and delights without giving too much pause. However, these are plays which, in the tradition of the carnivalesque, probe at the fabric of society, especially the hierarchies they contain.

The histories and tragedies are equally interested in both the idea of identity and society and where we, as individuals, sit within it. Coriolanus is a man who appears to no longer know himself when returning to Rome from yet another battle. In doing so his name changes throughout the play, beginning as Caius Marcius, before he becomes Coriolanus in honour of his defeat of Corioli. He is a man with three names, yet struggles to confirm his identity as absolute, fragmented and seeking to become the 'author of himself' (*Coriol.*, V, iii, 36). At the end of the play, he is quite literally fragmented as the angry mob of his enemy tear him limb from limb. The play itself is littered with metonymy where the head, the heart, the arms and legs of society are spoken about as separate and distinct entities. This is not a particularly subtle metaphor, but characters struggling to find both themselves and their place in society, at risk of a total loss of identity, abound.

Hamlet is a prince without a throne and a son without a father. He is neither child nor man and rejects the traditional routes presented to him, including the love of Ophelia. Macbeth realises, 'To know my deed 'twere best not know myself' (*Macb.*, II, ii, 74), unable to confront what he has become. Lear and Othello are not only blind to the true ways of those around them but also of themselves, only finding their true selves in tragedy.

Psychoanalytical readings of the plays that look at the idea of the fragmented self can be immensely rewarding, with characters representing different parts of the whole self. *Hamlet*, for example, has many different components, with the ghost of the old Hamlet, Laertes and Fortinbras all representative of Hamlet's troubled mind. This is something which productions have made bold choices with, opting to present it as a one-man show to emphasise his fragmentation and his alienation from his family and society. The tension between the individual and society is also at the heart of this, as it is when he explores familial relationships – especially those between father and daughter. The message though is a powerful one and the youthful and individual desires of Romeo and Juliet are disruptive and potentially damaging to the world in which they live, despite the eventual harmony they bring. Equally, the mature passion of Antony and Cleopatra disdains the needs of the empire in which they lead – a concept which brings us back to the fragmented Coriolanus, ripped apart by those representatives of society before he could rip society to pieces in his quest for himself.

Romantic and mixed-gender relationships

With men at the heart of the plays, the concerns around identity and societal roles often revolve around these masculine concerns. Issues around gender are hotly debated in the writing of Shakespeare and the interplay and relationships between the sexes are often instrumental to the action. Emma Smith argues that how we see Shakespeare's relationship to women in particular, reflects significantly on us, and if we as a society decide he is a misogynist then this reflects badly on how we see ourselves.[6] After all, if we see his work as important (something we

---

6   Emma Smith, 'Taming of the Shrew', *Approaching Shakespeare* [podcast] (9 November 2012). Available at: https://podcasts.ox.ac.uk/taming-shrew-0.

clearly do), what does that say about us? However, it is not simply his presentation of women which is of interest to us, but his presentation of masculinity and the relationships we have with those of the opposite sex.

The position of women during the Renaissance

During the Renaissance, women still experienced the constraints we have come to recognise in traditional patriarchal systems. Ownership of property and personal liberties was limited and women were frequently confined to the domestic sphere; something we see reflected in Shakespeare, with even Lady Macbeth's language indicating the difference in gender roles – the warrior Macbeth speaks in terms of daggers whilst she talks in terms of knives (associated in the realms of the domestic). However, women were as likely to be literate as men and class expectations were as significant to their position as their gender. Property and wealth were linked to upper class women, hence the importance of marriage in maintaining estates and accumulating the power associated with such. However, it is important not to forget that for half a century a woman had been ruler of England, and whilst women were relatively powerless, it is important to consider the anxieties in terms of gender roles Shakespeare presents, and avoid blanket statements about women in this period. Shakespeare had something to say around gender – and his audience, much like the audiences which predated him, were interested to know what.

Gender in Shakespeare

I would like to look at this specifically though the lens of *The Taming of the Shrew* as the gender relationships in this play could perhaps colour our own relationship with the rest of his texts. Certainly, one of my Year 9 groups, having looked already at gender roles in *Romeo and Juliet* and *Much Ado About Nothing*, found the relationship between Katherina and Petruchio rather disturbing to say the least and it made them completely reconsider their earlier readings of the other plays in terms of gender. In this play we have everything, from domineering father, the renaming of a woman to signify control and loss of identity in marriage, and out-and-out abuse with sleep deprivation and starvation to bring compliance from our female subject. Reading this with modern eyes certainly strips it of its more comedic elements and it is interesting to see fewer productions of this play circulating in modern times. Katherina's final speech (I too find it difficult not to award her preferred name) often forms the crux of how we read the play and if we see this as a final submission of the female sex then it is hard to read the play as one that is not highly problematic. In the longest speech of the play, she says:

> Fie, fie, unknit that threatening unkind brow, And dart not scornful glances from those eyes, To wound thy lord, thy king, thy governor: It blots thy beauty as frosts do bite the meads, Confounds thy fame as whirlwinds shake fair buds, And in no sense is meet or amiable. A woman mov'd is like a fountain troubled, Muddy, ill-seeming, thick, bereft of beauty; And while it is so, none so dry or thirsty Will deign to sip or touch one drop of it. Thy husband is thy lord, thy life, thy keeper, Thy head, thy sovereign; one that cares for thee, And for thy maintenance commits his body To painful labour both by sea and land, To watch the night in storms, the day in cold, Whilst thou liest warm at home, secure and safe; And craves no other tribute at thy hands But love, fair looks, and true obedience; Too little payment for so great a debt. Such duty as the subject owes the prince, Even such a woman oweth to her husband; And when she is froward, peevish, sullen, sour, And not obedient to his honest will, What is she but a foul contending rebel And graceless traitor to her loving lord?– I am asham'd that women are so simple To offer war where they should kneel for peace, Or seek for rule, supremacy, and sway, When they are bound to serve, love, and obey. Why are our bodies soft and weak and smooth, Unapt to toil and trouble in the world, But that our soft conditions and our hearts Should well agree with our external parts? Come, come, you froward and unable worms, My mind hath been as big as one of yours, My heart as great, my reason haply more, To bandy word for word and frown for frown; But now I see our lances are but straws, Our strength as weak, our weakness past compare, That seeming to be most which we indeed least are. Then vail your stomachs, for it is no boot, And place your hands below your husband's foot: In token of which duty, if he please, My hand is ready; may it do him ease.
>
> (*Tam. Shr.*, V, ii, 137–180)

If we read this as a call to subservience, then the idea of *Kate's* taming will forever be woven into our reading of the play. If, however, as others have suggested, what we are actually seeing is Katherina's declaration of independence then we will read this speech very differently. She has finally found a voice, something which she had little control over earlier in the play, having become 'Renown'd in Padua for her scolding tongue' (*Tam. Shr.*, I, ii, 101). In the play she is afforded few lines at the start, and we are given to imagine her as communicating using inarticulate grunts and screams as she fails to express her thoughts in a cohesive way. Her words at the end of the play, when she is finally given an articulate and astute voice, are as much for the husbands in the group as the wives; a lesson to all to consider the *war* they may offer in their relationships. This is perhaps most closely aligned to the lessons metered out to the men – Falstaff and Ford – who are schooled on their foolishness with humiliation in their pursuit of the women in *The Merry Wives of Windsor*. Dame Ellen Terry, the actor famed for her performances of Shakespeare's women, said Shakespeare's women were 'wonderful' and asks if we had ever wondered 'how much we all, and women especially, owe to Shakespeare for his vindication of women in these fearless, high-spirited, resolute and intelligent heroines?'[7] Few are more fearless that Katherina as she stands before us and presents her choice. Our 'shrew' in *The Taming of the Shrew* shows her wit and intelligence throughout the play as she spars with Petruchio, finding new articulation and control of her sharp tongue by the end, his attempts to seemingly silence her in fact leading to her displaying her skills as an orator. It is no accident, one would suppose, that she has the final word. However, in *Women of Will*, Tina Packer argues that Katherina has been silenced throughout and regards her final lines as one of total submission.[8]

But if we look at female roles in their totality, as opposed to isolated to individual works, we will see Katherina echoes the characters of Beatrice in *Much Ado About Nothing* who is revered for her quick wit and eloquence, or Hermia and Helena in *A Midsummer Night's Dream* who openly court men and defy their parents, or Portia in *The Merchant of Venice*; beautiful, wealthy and resourceful. Equally, in his sonnets Shakespeare talks of 'the marriage of true minds' and how he will not insult his love with 'false compare'.[9] These are not lovers who are

---

7   Ellen Terry, 'The Triumphant Women'. In *Four Lectures on Shakespeare*, ed. Christopher St John (London: Martin Hopkinson, 1932), p. 81.

8   Tina Packer, *Women of Will: The Remarkable Evolution of Shakespeare's Female Characters* (New York: Vintage Books, 2016), p. x.

9   William Shakespeare, Sonnet 116 and Sonnet 130. Available at: https://www.poetryfoundation.org/poems/45106/sonnet-116-let-me-not-to-the-marriage-of-true-minds and https://www.poetryfoundation.org/poems/45108/sonnet-130-my-mistress-eyes-are-nothing-like-the-sun.

submissive and easily won. Fathers who try to decide on their daughters' fates either end with tragedy or are overthrown to comedic ends. Cleopatra is a female ruler who strides like a colossus over her domain and weakens even the mighty Antony and the Rome he represents with her femininity. The women in his plays can be seen as powerful as much as they can be read as powerless.

That is not to say Shakespeare was a campaigner for gender equality (something which can confuse students who tend to either see misogyny or a champion to the cause) and certainly there is a lot to be read about his presentation of women in his texts, not least in Sonnet 144 where the dark lady is presented as the temptress; impure and luring him from his other love (interestingly often argued to be male, representing either aspects of sexuality or fraternity). Certainly, my arguments about Katherina's freedom of speech did little to convince my class that their relationship was a positive one, and much that they had suspected about their view of Shakespeare from their reading of the Hero–Claudio relationship in *Much Ado About Nothing* remained unchallenged. But to simply cast Shakespeare as either an early feminist or an outright misogynist would be to potentially miss the opportunity to explore the questions he raised about gender roles, at a time when questions about power and gender were very much at the fore with Elizabeth on the throne. Just as with everything in literature, Shakespeare provides a way for us to enter into these debates and provides an opportunity for students to consider how we might interpret these plays in a much more nuanced way than *women had no power, stayed in the home* and *Shakespeare supports the patriarchy*. I think saying it is complicated would be right here.

His concerns around gender often focus on male/female relationships, but he is equally concerned with questions around masculinity – especially masculinity in a changing and shifting world. From considering the role of the soldier in *Coriolanus* and *Macbeth* to examining fraternal relationships in *The Two Noble Kinsmen* and *Romeo and Juliet*, what it means to be a man is very much up for discussion and different presentations of this run throughout his plays. Romeo offers an alternative masculinity to those presented by his peers and *Hamlet*, *Othello* and *Henry V* all centre on how these men find their place in their worlds. Again, often more questions are raised than answered, but as we explore these ideas with our students we offer them opportunities to engage in discussions much wider than these texts.

Sexuality

When Carol Ann Duffy talks about her own reimagining of Anne Hathaway in her poem of that title, she presents Shakespeare as a sexual man.[10] In her poem she explores the mutually pleasurable sexual relationship between the two, and this is something she takes not only from biographical details of their lives, albeit ones which had long periods of separation, but from his writing. He is the man who wrote poetry whilst others 'dribbled' prose, and it is from his writing that she draws this inference. As much as Shakespeare writes of romantic love and gender relationships, he writes about sexual relationships. From bawdy double entendres in plays such as *Romeo and Juliet*, to the heartbreaking melodies of Ophelia in *Hamlet* (Act IV, sc. v), and deeply passionate sexual relationships in *Antony and Cleopatra* and *Othello*, he is as keen to explore this aspect of human interaction as he is to examine others.

Shakespeare certainly enjoys a pun too, toying with innuendo as well as more serious explorations of the consequences of unfettered sexual desire, untampered by the bonds of marriage. Perhaps most strikingly we can see this in *A Midsummer Night's Dream*, a play very much reimagined by the Victorians as one which was both suitable and accessible to children, with the promise of magical folk and fairy tales. However, the implied sexual relationships in the play are complex, with partner swapping, the aggressive sexual desire of the women in the play who are prepared to submit or dominate to their satisfaction, and even bestiality in the form of the Titania and Bottom interlude. As Titania draws Bottom to her 'flowery bed' and kisses his 'large donkey ears' (*Mids. N D.*, IV, i, 1 and 4), the performance can either underplay or emphasise the implications for the audience. Whilst what would be shown on the stage would have been limited due to censorship laws, the connotations here are strong and would not be lost on the audience.

This is not to say these relationships are not unproblematic ones. As much as Helena, seeking to be beaten by her love interest if that means he will love her, talks of a particular desire, it also speaks volumes about the gender roles too, once again reminding us of the dominance and submission in plays such as *The Taming of the Shrew*. Sexuality and sexual violence are always something we need to reflect on in terms of how much to explore this in the classroom. It is a question we need to grapple with as teachers; there are both references to and actual rape which takes

---

10 Carol Ann Duffy, 'Anne Hathaway' in *The World's Wife* (New York: Macmillan, 1999), p. 24.

place within his stories, and we need to gauge how we approach this in terms of the maturity of our students and sensitivity of approach. In terms of references to sex, students often delight as they see the double meanings emerge at the start of *Romeo and Juliet*, as the servants draw their 'naked weapon,' but are understandably horrified at the further references to maids who will be thrust against the wall and 'maidenheads' (I, i, 29). Once they begin to examine the words of the Porter in *Macbeth* as he muses on the effect alcohol has on desire and the ability to do the deed, they are equally amused.

They are also often intrigued by the discussions around Shakespeare's own sexuality – especially those which emerge from studying Sonnet 20 – as the mystery of the man behind the art is always an appealing one, but this will remain for us to judge how far to explore what that tells us about the writer (something to approach with caution) as opposed to that of the form and context (advice to a younger man as opposed to one which reveals same-sex desire). But to study *Romeo and Juliet*, *Macbeth*, *Antony and Cleopatra* and *Much Ado About Nothing* (with the inclusion of 'nothing' often used during this period to signify the sexual organs, both piquing students' interest as well as setting them up for the focus of the play) without making reference to the more risqué elements would be to lose something. As always, though, in your curriculum you will need to make a decision about what to include, and when, in order to ensure students can engage with the most important elements of his writing without becoming derailed into supposition or concerns about the more adult themes.

How to teach it

Exploring themes is central to all we do in English literature, especially as we delve into conceptual understanding and the relevance of the text to the modern audience. We both want students to see the relevance of the texts to their daily lives, as well as to engage with the debates and discussions which surround the concepts, spanning not only Shakespeare's work but the work of many, many writers since.

One important thing to note is how quickly many of the themes which will be central to his plays are drawn out in the first scenes and speeches. So, if we were to look at the opening speech of *King Lear* we will see he introduces us to the division and disorder which will become the focus of the play, and Macbeth tells us immediately not to trust what we are about to see, plunging us into uncertainty and unnatural events, where duplicity is the order of the day with the witches' line 'fair is foul' (*Macb.*, I, i, 9). These are the main points to focus on as we then see the action unfold and a close study of openings, once students are familiar with plot and character, can yield a great deal of insight into what these themes are.

In this case study from Heidi Drake, a deputy head of English in a school in Essex, she explains how she approaches the idea of power and leadership in her curriculum across the key stages and how 'golden threads' are explored by her students over time.

I have always considered myself to be, at least in part, a new histor-icist. This is fortunate considering the emphasis placed on context by exam boards at both GCSE and A level. I studied history up until the end of my first year at university and the Plantagenets up to the Glorious Revolution had become my main area of study in English history. This is very useful when it comes to putting together the Shakespeare element of our curriculum.

Of course, Shakespeare wrote different plays about different things, but he was also a man of his time. It is likely that he had read at least translated extracts of Machiavelli's *The Prince* and, as a grammar schoolboy, he would most likely have read classical texts on govern-ance. Governance was also the hot topic of the chattering classes at the time Shakespeare was writing. Reading Hadfield's *Shakespeare and Renaissance Politics* and Greenblatt's *Tyrant: Shakespeare on Politics* really crystallised for me how this was a thread running through Shakespeare's works and one that you see developing and changing over time as the political landscape, and Shakespeare him-self, changed.[11] Identifying this as an *expert* is one thing; using that knowledge to support and extend *novices* is another matter entirely. But Shakespeare's explorations of governance and what makes a good ruler/leader have become a central feature (and a key *big ques-tion*) in the construction of our literature curriculum in Key Stage 5.

---

11 Andrew Hadfield, *Shakespeare and Renaissance Politics* (London: Bloomsbury, 2003); Stephen Greenblatt, *Tyrant: Shakespeare on Politics* (New York: W.W. Norton & Company, 2019).

Shakespeare is introduced to our students in Year 7 in our Heroes and Villains unit. This includes extracts from *Henry V* and *Richard III* as key areas of study. Both the speeches we look at – 'Once more unto the breach dear friends' (*Hen. V.*, III, i, 1–34) and 'Now is the winter of our discontent' (*Rich. III*, I, i, 1) – are easier for the students to understand when looked at from a new historicist perspective. The contexts of both the kings themselves and how they relate to Shakespeare's times and intentions are explored explicitly (links to the history curriculum are helpful here, as in so many places in literature curricula). The students are often fascinated to discover that many of Shakespeare's contemporaries spent time in the Tower of London due to what they wrote (telling them the story of the production of *Richard II* that was commissioned in support of Essex's rebellion also leads to some excitement!). When they have a grasp of what is being discussed (and you need to be wary of assumptions here – it took quite a long time for a few of my students to understand what the breach was in terms of siege warfare, which took me a little by surprise) we move on to modelling the how, introducing key tier 3 vocabulary[12] before bringing all this knowledge together into an exploration of why; at first, using oracy skills before moving on to producing this in writing.

Year 8 move on to looking at a whole play: *Richard III*. They look at how power and the desire for it can corrupt those seeking it and the society around them. Good governance, of course, does not just affect individuals but society and the fabric of the state itself. They also explicitly, and importantly, consider how form and structure support this meaning to be created at scene, act and whole text level. Why are the plays structured in this way? Why this scene there? Why does Shakespeare mention how dark or light it is in his plays? Why do people say who has just arrived on stage when we can see them? Considerations of the context Shakespeare was writing for (the Globe Theatre at 2 p.m., cue scripts, etc.) are not just interesting, but they also make it clear why the plays are written in this way and discourage students from talking/writing about the text as a book instead of as a play.

---

12 Tier 3 words are those which are specific to a subject; for example, *metonymy* in English or *radius* in mathematics.

Of course, Shakespeare doesn't just look at governance at a national scale but at a domestic and societal level as well. In Year 9 we explore *Romeo and Juliet* in this way (as well as by reviewing the concept of tragedy), feeding in explorations of masculinity and power at this stage. This enables us to provide our students with a framework that shows that some of the concerns of Shakespeare's era remain with us today. In preparing *Romeo and Juliet* in this way I am indebted to the work of Matt Pinkett and Mark Roberts.[13] We also take the opportunity to introduce the concept of dichotomies to the students. We don't explicitly link this to structuralism/post-structuralism, but the building blocks of a different critical framework are put in place to develop later in Key Stages 4 and 5. At GCSE, teachers are allowed to teach any text from the specification. At the moment that means either *Macbeth* or *The Tempest*. The *golden thread* of what makes a good ruler/leader continues with both plays exploring this explicitly. The approaches followed through Key Stage 3 mean that by the time we start Shakespeare (autumn term of Year 11) our students are adept scholars of early modern drama and how it is constructed for meaning.

By focusing on Elizabethan-era plays before moving on to Jacobean, the changes in how Shakespeare approaches the theme of governance in his plays can be made clear to the students – this helps them to contextualise those changes as they match with the chronology of what happened when, which I believe serves to reduce the cognitive load somewhat. The two GCSE options are very different from the plays looked at in Key Stage 3 in terms of meanings and the students are then more able to think of Shakespeare as an artist whose opinion and/or contexts changed over time rather than one set thing. There are *Shakespeares* rather than one unchangeable Shakespeare.

Currently, at A level we study *Hamlet* (although at other times we have looked at *Othello* or *King Lear*). Whilst *Hamlet* loops back in Shakespeare's chronology, it clearly links well with the thread of governance in both the political and domestic spheres, and from this perspective connects particularly well with both *Macbeth* and *The*

---

13 Matt Pinkett and Mark Roberts, *Boys Don't Try? Rethinking Masculinity in Schools* (Abingdon: Routledge, 2019).

Tempest. Gaining the knowledge to explore all this with the students has necessitated background research and reading. Good subject knowledge is key when it comes to approaching Shakespeare and I have used the invaluable resources of the Royal Shakespeare Company and Shakespeare's Globe even through lockdown. However, good subject knowledge is not enough and must be coupled with pedagogical knowledge. There are few resources that do both to a high enough level but one that does is *Ready to Teach: Macbeth.*[14]

I firmly believe that finding threads that run through all the Shakespeare texts you cover is important. It helps the students link form and context to meaning as they see it happen repeatedly. It helps them hone their skills on pulling these linked threads and move on to spotting their own. And, in my own experience, it has increased enjoyment of and engagement with Shakespeare's work.

Heidi clearly believes that exploring these big ideas and returning to them in the five of seven years that students study the work of Shakespeare, is an important element to what she is doing. Building conceptual understanding which weaves together aspects of context, allusion and character are key to what she wants her students to understand.

Similarly in this second case study, Lyndsey Steed, an English teacher working at the West Exe School in Exeter, explains how they have taken a more thematic approach to the teaching of Shakespeare across a unit, having been prompted by some of their reflections from the 2020–2021 COVID-19 lockdown situation to try something new. Instead of a linear reading of the texts, she takes a wider perspective and traces themes across the learning sequence which has so far yielded good results for the students.

---

14 Stuart Pryke and Amy Staniforth, *Ready to Teach: Macbeth: A Compendium of Subject Knowledge, Resources and Pedagogy* (Woodbridge: John Catt Educational, 2020).

With lockdown providing the opportunity to revise schemes of learning, I took advantage of my experience as an examiner to redesign how we teach Shakespeare for GCSE literature. My rationale was to exchange a linear study of the text to a thematic approach. By doing this I felt we would be better able to prepare our students for the exam task they will encounter: *How does Shakespeare present [character/theme] in this extract and the play as a whole?*

When studying the play in a linear fashion, it is largely impossible for students to answer this style of question because for the first few weeks, they haven't got the knowledge of the play as a complete text. This means it is only in the latter stages of the unit that we can address the skills of linking the ideas and structuring them into a successful response. This also creates the situation where, in the later weeks of the scheme, we can find ourselves as teachers realising that we've only just started Act III when we're rapidly approaching the point where we need to complete the final assessment. By focusing on a thematic approach, we can still cover the entire play but by focusing on what is necessary. By streamlining the content in this way, we reduce cognitive overload and enable our students to succeed with Shakespeare and, ideally, take actual enjoyment from the play too.

The first phase of my planning involved identifying and sequencing the themes to build a template for what the students will do week by week. The first week focuses on the general contextual background of Shakespeare's life and times. This includes reference to Shakespeare's classical education through producing the thematic lens of Greek love for students to consider as they work through the play. This establishment week also includes a guided viewing of the Baz Luhrmann production so that students have both encountered the play as a whole text and seen it in performance. After this, the scheme develops in two-week thematic blocks: weeks 2–3 – society; weeks 4–5 – gender; weeks 6–7 – relationships; weeks 8–9 – the metaphysical; weeks 10–12 – revision/assessment/feedback and reflection.

For the next phase, I had to track these themes across the text, drawing the essential extracts to include in a specifically designed workbook (that will also serve as a revision tool) to accompany the scheme's PowerPoint. Pedagogically, I then thought about the tasks that would facilitate students to learn the material and the skills necessary to respond to the exam question. These included opportunities for close reading of the text with short extracts to limit the amount of information that students receive in one go, with: guided tasks to help them identify and annotate key quotes, techniques and ideas; language analysis, and scaffolds to develop their ideas in greater detail; modelled paragraphing, following an *I do–We do–You do* format to demonstrate how the skills look when brought together and to develop their confidence in communicating their ideas in the first week. Then, in the second week, I introduce an independent extended writing task with live marking; Cornell Notes are used to develop students' ability to retrieve contextual information and to introduce higher level, conceptual thinking.[15] Over the course of the 12-week unit the scaffolding is gradually withdrawn to enable students to develop independence and confidence.

So far, we have taught the first half of this new scheme and the general feeling within my department is that this approach has condensed and clarified the play in a way that makes the delivery of the lessons more successful than a linear approach. All students of all abilities have been able to engage with higher-level concepts and, from the very start of the unit, to begin linking key events, characters and ideas in a way that they would not have been able to in studying scene by scene, act by act.

Lyndsey and her team have thought carefully about the benefits of tracing themes across a play before they begin the closer analysis required for the exam. This broader perspective means that so far they have found that the conceptual thinking of their students has improved by using this approach, moving them beyond a simple focus on narrative sequencing. Students still experience the text as a whole as they first encounter the text in performance through the film adaptation, leaving them in a strong position to explore the concepts and the language used to convey them.

This is an approach I favoured myself, using both cinematic and stage performance and summaries as a form of cold read we may be more

---

15 Cornell Notes are a system of notes developed at Cornell University in the 1950s by Walter Pauk. More details can be found here https://lsc.cornell.edu/wp-content/uploads/2015/10/Cornell-Note_Taking-System.pdf.

familiar with when studying prose texts. Students then have a clear understanding of the text as a whole piece and as we delve deeper into the text, layering the understanding around key extracts and themes, enabling them to then respond to the big questions posed by the text as well as those posed by the exam board. Outcomes for my students who encountered the play in this way were frequently better than those who were still struggling to grasp plot and character, having examined the play in a more linear fashion. In addition, by approaching the plays thematically, there are frequent opportunities to return to key elements of plot, ensuring spaced practice and retrieval is well embedded, as well as extending student understanding beyond basic plot points.

These themes also provide a useful frame for sequencing the study of the play. Asking, 'How does Shakespeare want to present love in *Romeo and Juliet*? Or what is the significance of the supernatural in *Macbeth*?' can help to introduce students to a more discursive approach to their studies, as well as provide a wider picture of what you want to look at in the play. This is useful when students need to be able to make links across a text as opposed to seeing it as a linear process, and will enable them to make connections between extracts and quotes throughout the play an important aspect of the exam and for their understanding.

It can also allow you to trace themes across the curriculum with other texts; exploring the significance of the supernatural in Shakespeare can be equally important when looking at Dickens, and issues around gender or power or conflict will be relevant to a huge range of other texts too. Immediately we are thinking beyond the teaching of Shakespeare and considering how his work fits into literary traditions and the relationship we may have with his work when writing back. Another way to approach this is by introducing some of the themes which will be explored later, via reading other texts. The narrative poem *Long Way Down* by Jason Reynolds is an effective way to introduce ideas of revenge, rivalry and masculinity prior to examining these themes in *Romeo and Juliet*.[16] Equally, looking at non-fiction to begin to discuss the universality, or otherwise, of his plays can create links and connections to real-world situations.

---

16 Jason Reynolds, *Long Way Down* (London: Faber & Faber, 2018).

Applying it to the classroom

- Decide on the key themes you are interested in exploring with your students and make it explicit. Trace these across the play once they have understood the plot, character and overall structure.

- Discuss how these themes do, or do not, relate to your students' lives now, making use of non-fiction articles. For example, when studying *Romeo and Juliet*, I would make use of non-fiction articles on the topic of arranged marriage, knife crime and the pressure to conform to gendered stereotypes.

- Highlight how these big ideas are presented in other works of fiction too, including non-Shakespearean ones. Issues of gender, power and identity appear in many texts and links between texts such as *Lord of the Flies* and *Macbeth* become a powerful vehicle for students to explore these ideas. Poetry that examines these same ideas can be used to prompt retrieval and extend the conversation further. These often worked well either as starter tasks in a lesson or to prime students for the analysis we would go on to do.

- Big questions can provide a useful frame for the learning, to link themes together and support retention and make learning more likely to adhere with their other knowledge. Thesis statements at the start of essays are good ways to lead into conceptual exploration of the texts. Considering how these themes link to context and the language used to present them. Using key quotes to link the ideas together is another way to ensure that students will be able to recall these quickly and retain this knowledge for later use.

- Model thesis statements (the opening argument of an essay), for students, either live via a visualiser or using a whiteboard. Where exemplars are used, dissect these with your students and consider how they are establishing a conceptual or thematic approach. Give them a range of examples and use the *I do–We do–You do* approach to first show them the steps to constructing a response, discussing and constructing it collaboratively, before moving into the independent stage.

- Oral rehearsal can also be a good way to ensure these ideas can be retained; giving students time to discuss the line of argument they will take can be powerful before they put pen to paper.

+ Cluster retrieval practice around themes to build strong schemas focused on the themes, as opposed to characters and scenes. Ask students to refer to quotes and moments which relate to ideas about conflict or love. This is more likely to be retained than if students see them as disparate pieces of information.

+ Model ways to organise this knowledge, using mind maps or graphic organisers which scaffold students' understanding by giving them some of the details and prompts. This can also be used generatively or to scaffold revision.[17]

+ Use visual images as well as performance to support a range of learners to make links between the themes and the text. Images of the crown to represent the theme of kingship or power, for example, can be an important way to ensure students can understand where these ideas reoccur.

+ Circle back to the key themes you want to teach, giving students the opportunity to revisit and revaluate their importance and development.

---

17 Generative learning is a process by which we create new meaning. Logan Fiorella and Richard Mayer found eight strategies that support this process most effectively, including mapping and summarising. For more information, see: Zoe Enser and Mark Enser, *Fiorella & Mayer's Generative Learning in Action* (Woodbridge: John Catt Educational, 2020).

Chapter 5

Bringing Forth His Language

Symbols, Motifs and the Musicality

it is a tale
Told by an idiot, full of sound and fury,
Signifying nothing.

(Macb., V, v, 26–28)

Why do they talk like that, Miss? It doesn't make any sense.

(pretty much every student taught for over 20 years)

The language of Shakespeare is perhaps one of the greatest barriers to most readers unfamiliar with the style, allusions and patterns. As much as we are told iambic pentameter mirrors patterns of speech, this was not how Elizabethans spoke – although, just as today, there were differences in register associated with different social groupings. *Thee* and *thou* seem alien to students who are used to prose that flows over the page relatively easily, but the barrier is especially true when we are talking about exploring his works with students who are perhaps not yet fully proficient in reading modern prose. There are also plenty of adults who will askew the pleasures of Shakespeare, finding his linguistic stylings impenetrable and simply not worth the effort. However, Shakespeare's language can be something of a leveller as it doesn't necessarily matter how proficient you may be at reading generally; all students (and indeed many adults) will stumble across his words and need to deploy a different approach to reading than they may be used to.

Why teach it?

With so many finding the language problematic, there is a temptation to strip some of the complexity away; to focus instead on summaries or modern adaptations which translate the ideas into a more familiar vernacular. There is, though, much to be gained by examining his choice of words as they appear, much as you would were you to be exploring a poem with the class; sometimes simply letting the intricacies of the language wash over you whilst you enjoy the musicality of the plays; other times we need to dig down and explore the real nitty-gritty of the language. *Getting it* can be really satisfying too, and a key light-bulb moment for me at school was seeing how unpicking meaning could be looked at like a puzzle to be solved, much in common with solving equations in maths or finding the pieces of an intricate jigsaw. It was edifying to be able to piece together meaning from what initially appeared to be a random collection of words.

Many argue that spending time reading and analysing his plays outside of performance is an exercise in artificiality but, as noted elsewhere, Shakespeare was not only concerned with stagecraft and performance, but his readership too. He was a published author in his lifetime and conscious crafting and revision to meet the needs of his readers are as important as those he made for his audience. Most importantly perhaps is that his use of poetry, imagery and musicality frequently stays with us, and lines from Shakespeare that linger in our mind and our everyday language remain due to their crafting. We want to allow students to have that opportunity too.

Exam board requirements aside, as mentioned previously the study of Shakespeare's language can be an enriching experience. It is not only about wading through to find meaning, but to enjoy the musicality of his rhymes, the joy to be found in his imagery and the ideas which he holds up for inspection in a brand-new way. We might feel overly familiar with lines such as 'it is the east, and Juliet is the sun!' (*Rom. & Jul.*, I, ii, 3), but to many of our students exploring the depth of what this metaphor could really convey is new and exciting. What is the significance of the east? Why the sun? What possible ways can we read that? What does it convey about Romeo's feelings at this moment? Is this a positive or negative perspective on someone he has (*literally*, as my students shout at me) just met? These thoughts might go through our mind in seconds but for our students having the opportunity to analyse this in-depth and really get to the heart of the meaning behind such a well-known and oft-parodied line, can give them a new appreciation of how seemingly simple language can convey so much. Just as with the teaching of poetry, I often find my students' responses to prose text, especially when they are looking for patterns in the imagery writers are using, improve significantly after we have studied Shakespeare – and this is something we can start at Key Stage 3 and even earlier. With novels, students will frequently focus primarily on the feelings of the characters as if they are real people, looking to analyse the text in terms of how they related to that person. When we study Shakespeare or poetry this element is often stripped away. This means that we perhaps have to be even more explicit as we take them through the process that will lead to their own response, but it also has the added benefit of the language being laid bare in a way which the obsession with characterisation and plot in novels just doesn't. This means when we return to the prose texts, I find students often notice increasingly insightful things around the language choices, as opposed to racing through the words on the page to see what happens next. Andrew Atherton, a director of research and academic enrichment, as well as a teacher of English, talks here about how poeticising Shakespeare is important in his classroom.

A perennial cry of the classroom when teaching Shakespeare, one all too familiar to any English teacher, is some variation of: 'But Sir, this doesn't make any sense! What is he talking about?!' Stood at the front of the room, awash with the majesty of a soliloquy from *Hamlet*, we ask ourselves why our students don't feel the way we do. There is a great moment in the TV show *Upstart Crow* that offers an answer to this very question.[1] Here, David Mitchell's Shakespeare complains to his wife that he can't attend an upcoming performance because, he says, 'Two tunnels which lie beneath the bridge be blocked.' His wife, Anne, looks on in utter confusion. Frustrated, Mitchell's Shakespeare proclaims, 'Two tunnels? Beneath a bridge? Anyone?' before wearily explaining: 'Nose, my loves. Nose! I've told Burbage that my nose be snotted and I would not work this week or next.' Wearied but somehow not surprised, Anne asks, 'Why didn't you just say nose?' to which Shakespeare responds, 'It's what I do.'

---

1   *Upstart Crow*, dir. Matt Lipsey and Richard Boden [TV series] (BBC, 2016–2020).

When I first saw this scene, much to the confusion of my own non-teacher wife, I just could not stop laughing. It seemed to me to encapsulate exactly the issue that so many of our students find with Shakespeare: it just doesn't seem to make sense! But why not exactly?

As played with in this moment from *Upstart Crow*, what often confuses in Shakespeare is the deliberate ambiguity of so much of his writing; the way in which, paraphrasing Emily Dickinson, he speaks at a slant.[2] In other words, what we find difficult about Shakespeare's language is that it is so often poetry and always poetic. Yet, despite this, in my experience anyway and myself very much included, we don't always teach it as poetry and students don't often think of it as poetry. Embedding this subtle but powerful conceptual shift in the way in which we frame Shakespeare to our students, and the way we plan, makes a big difference. *It's not that it doesn't make sense*, we should cry – *it's poetry!* This simple recognition has the potential to liberate how students approach Shakespeare, and how they, and we, conceptualise the difficulty and frustrations they will inevitably encounter when studying his plays. Students often, perhaps even happily, struggle through poetry because they have a certain degree of anticipation that poetry does not open itself up automatically: it takes work, effort and sustained thought, and that is OK. However, they do not necessarily have this expectation with a play, even Shakespeare, and so find the inevitable struggle a little more unpalatable. By reframing the kind of intellectual engagement we expect to have with Shakespeare, and by foregrounding its obvious poeticism, we prime students for the kind of encounter they might expect to have. We rationalise and schematise this difficulty. In my own teaching of Shakespeare, and with all of the above in mind, I make a conscious and deliberate effort to poeticise Shakespeare right from the outset. Here, then, are a couple of quick strategies I've deployed in my own teaching of Shakespeare – perhaps familiar to the poetry classroom but maybe not always to teaching Shakespeare.

---

2   Emily Dickinson, 'Tell all the truth but tell it slant'. In *The Poems of Emily Dickinson: Reading Edition*, ed. Ralph W. Franklin (Cambridge, MA: The Belknap Press of Harvard University Press, 1998). Available at: https://www.poetryfoundation.org/poems/56824/tell-all-the-truth-but-tell-it-slant-1263.

Crush the scene

One such idea is what we might call *crushing the scene*. Here, we condense and curate those images within the scene or moment we most want our students to be thinking about. We might do this just by listing the words or by blocking out what we don't want to be seen. The reason this works so well for poetry is because it acknowledges that any single image or word could be cracked open to reveal within it a rich vein of linguistic depth that students can mine. But when we begin to foreground the poeticism of Shakespeare, much the same is true for his plays. We can use this to shape and direct student attention, but also to feel the stylistic weight of each image. We might do this to preface class discussion or to frame the poetic landscape of a specific moment within the play.

Resonant reading

When teaching poetry, we are quick to admit the vital role that authentic student response plays in generating and shaping meaning. Yet this is perhaps slightly lost sometimes when turning our attention to other kinds of text. Resonant reading is a great and really simple way to get this back with Shakespeare. Either whilst watching a performance or just when reading out a section of the play, we begin by alerting our students to the fact that what we're about to listen to or watch is incredibly rich and so we need to pay really close attention to the words we're about to hear. It's important that for this strategy students don't have access to a written copy of the play. Once we get to the end of whatever section we wanted to focus on, we ask students to jot down anything at all that they just heard that resonated with them. It might be a word or image or idea. What we're looking for, you explain, are splinters of the scene that caught their attention – even if they can't remember exactly what was said. We now have a room full of images or words that for whatever reason somehow resonated with your students. We now repeat this process, replaying the same scene a couple more times and continuing to gather together these resonances. This is like reading in slow motion as we carefully attend to what we're hearing, with students not looking to the language as a vehicle for plot but rather, in itself, something to dwell on and in. After each listening cycle we can then begin to use this material to interrogate these resonances: why do you think you remembered that? What was it about that word or image that struck you as interesting? Have we encountered any other similar words in the play?

Imagery threading

This is a strategy I use a lot when teaching an anthology of poetry in order to tease out connections across poems, but it works just as well for an imagery-rich text like a Shakespeare play. We begin by deciding on a motif that runs throughout the play – in *Macbeth*, for example, it might be blood or darkness. Now, we collectively gather together specific lines or images that relate to this motif from across the play and collate these lines next to one another, perhaps with a Word document or by quickly jotting them down. With our raw material, effectively lines of poetry all threaded together by a single motif, we can begin to interrogate in what sequence we might place these lines together and why. What juxtapositions might help to tease meaning out of the images? Are there parallels or stark contrasts across the selected images? Once we have the lines in some kind of sequence, we can then analyse the transformed text just like a poem, considering the imagery in its own right, but also the story it reveals about a given character or the thematic development of the play.

This process of poeticising Shakespeare opens up so many pedagogic and imaginative possibilities, since, by foregrounding the poetry of his plays, we have at our disposal a whole repertoire of strategies that might otherwise remain confined to the teaching of verse. Yet, perhaps even more significantly, it helps to reconceptualise for our students just why Shakespeare is difficult; that this is not something to shy away from but, like with poetry, to embrace and celebrate.

Overcoming those initial barriers of language and finding a way in which students can engage with his writing without losing the possibilities his language presents to us, is a key aim in Atherton's teaching of the text here. To move students beyond their initial trepidation when confronted with something so unfamiliar, but still retaining the joys of examining motifs and symbols (more on that later), is a delicate balance and one we should be cautious not to rush through.

What is it?

As teachers of English and literature across all phases are the audience for this book, I don't think it is necessary to dwell too long on explanations around terms such as *metaphor* and *simile*. However, Shakespeare uses a range of linguistic devices in his writing, as well as structural ones, so it is worth just clarifying how some of these are used in his work. Some things to look out for are:

+ Motifs and symbols are rife in his work. As Matthew Lynch shows (see page 104), the bird motif in *Macbeth* is significant, baut equally animals appear in other plays as symbols, such as the lion or the lamb. Light and darkness and colours also take on a symbolic relevance and exploring these with your students can be a powerful way to consider how language, especially when considered in relation to semantic fields, can direct our readings.

+ Repetition, doubling, parallels and echoes. Patterns in language, especially doubling and tripling (see pages 75 and 120) are a hallmark of Shakespeare. It is possible to trace images and motifs across his work through his precise use of language and often it feels like words flutter around the text. His obsession with twins and parallels extends to his language. He also uses inversions, flipping around phrases in order to either create humour where characters parallel each other in speech, destabilise the reader or to create tension; for example, as we hear Macbeth echo the words of the witches as we first meet him – 'As fair and foul a day I have not seen' (*Macb.*, I, iii, 1) – or Prince Hamlet mocking the meaning, or meaninglessness, of language throughout the play.

+ Patterns of language also work across his plays, and once again create the sense of not only a style (something which some critics take much joy in unpicking to reveal the influence of his collaborators), but also recognition from the audience as they recognise the images from other plays resonating with them.

+ Metonymy is a type of metaphor where we replace a part with the whole. Perhaps the most common example we will see is where the word *crown* or *throne* replaces the idea of ascent to the throne. These are used regularly throughout our everyday language and, as with many metaphors, we may barely notice them. However, Shakespeare extends the use of these in his plays.

* Rhetoric has its roots deep in the world of Plato and his contemporaries. The art of persuasion makes significant use of figurative language (see examples from leaders and politicians over the ages, including Martin Luther King Jr), and has three key approaches in its appeal to the audience: *pathos*, *logos*, and *ethos*.[3] Pathos is where the speaker or writer aims to appeal to the emotions of the audience, and is deployed effectively many times in Shakespeare's work – for example, Marc Antony's oration over Caesar's body in *Julius Caesar* (III, ii, 79–202) or Lady Macbeth's pitiful figure in the sleepwalking scene (*Macb.*, IV, v). Logos focuses on logical argument, drawing on reasoning and presenting the facts of the matter to win favour. Ethos focuses on the speaker or writer's personal experience and expertise in the area which supplants that of his audience. Shakespeare's characters are seemingly adept at this approach, with everyone from Lady Macbeth to Julius Caesar probably displaying some of the most famous examples of rhetoric.[4] If students have a good understanding of this device, then not only can it support their understanding of key moments across a range of plays, it also supports their reading of non-fiction texts as well as considering their own writing which seeks to persuade or create a convincing argument.

Metre and rhyme

One of the often-cited things about Shakespeare's work is that it is written in iambic pentameter. Whilst he makes use of this metre, with its five metrical feet, each consisting of one short (or unstressed) syllable followed by one long (or stressed) syllable (for example 'Two *households*, both *alike* in *dignity*'[5]), it is simplistic to suggest this was the only way he

---

3 Martin Luther King Jr, *I Have a Dream* (New York: Harper One, 1991). Dr Martin Luther King Jr's famous speech makes use of a range of figurative language; both that associated with slavery and biblical images. King also employs aspects of all three rhetorical approaches as listed above.

4 Kim Ballard, 'Rhetoric, power and persuasion in Julius Caesar', *The British Library, Discovering Literature: Shakespeare & Renaissance* (15 March 2016). Available at: https://www.bl.uk/shakespeare/articles/rhetoric-power-and-persuasion-in-julius-caesar.

5 In this example you will see the line begin with the unstressed 'two', followed by the stressed 'households', then again an unstressed 'both' followed by the stressed 'alike'. These choices will encourage certain words to be stressed when spoken, whilst others will be spoken with a drop in the emphasis.

presented his work – although as a rule, characters who are *high-born* speak in iambic verse in his plays, whilst those of the lower classes speak in prose. There are some exceptions to be found, however. It is often thought that iambic pentameter mirrors the natural flow of speech or mimics the beat of a heart, making Shakespeare's work more memorable and appealing to something innate within us, but in 15th- and 16th-century poetry there was a wide variety of metre employed. However, the work of Shakespeare and Spenser seemed to have popularised its use, especially in poetry, and it quickly became prevalent.

But not all of Shakespeare's work was written in iambic pentameter, although his sonnets follow this form religiously. It is also important to remember that he wrote in prose, including one play, *The Merry Wives of Windsor*, written almost entirely in prose. However, Shakespeare also employs a range of other metres, once again indicating his deliberate crafting. The rhymes of the witches in *Macbeth* are probably the most interesting ones to explore with students once they have grasped the idea of iambic pentameter. The witches speak in something called *trochaic tetrameter*, a rhythm which places the stress on the syllable in exactly the opposite place to the iambic. There are also eight syllables as opposed to the ten which are used in iambic. This means that as they tell us 'fair is foul, and foul is fair' (*Macb.*, I, i, 9) the stresses fall on the opening word, representing in metre the very meaning of the words. This is often where students begin to conclude that this is clever stuff we are dealing with here. The natural rhythms of speech are inverted and we not only see but hear how unnatural these creatures are.

A note on his poetry

Many of Shakespeare's themes and ideas continue to be explored in his poetry. If you were to ask an Elizabethan audience about Shakespeare's work, they would most likely have talked about his poetry and not his plays. He was not only a writer of sonnets though, writing two narrative poems: *Venus and Adonis* in 1593, a text which was much available in print in his lifetime, and *The Rape of Lucrece* in 1594.[6] The latter is a story he references in his later plays, with 'Tarquin's ravishing strides' (*Macb.*, II, i, 55) leading Macbeth to the innocent Duncan's bedchamber, much as the abhorrent Sextus Tarquinius' lust for Lucrecia leads him to her room. Much like Macbeth, Tarquin is full of shame and guilt for his

---

6   William Shakespeare, *The Complete Works of Shakespeare* (London: Magpie Books, 1992).

actions, the line then foreshadowing the consequences which would await Macbeth. Tarquin was also known to be a bloody tyrant, once again preparing us for later events in the play.

Venus and Adonis is a tale of unrequited love, as the goddess Venus attempts to seduce the handsome young Adonis, who rejects her in favour of hunting. It is a narrative which contains comic and tragic events and is often considered to be the most likely of his works to first have been available in print. The poem explores ideas of love and is erotic at times, as well as including his observations on nature. This can make an interesting companion to some of his other writing around love, with clear parallels with *Romeo and Juliet*, *Love's Labour's Lost* and *A Midsummer Night's Dream*. It is written in iambic pentameter, and takes its source from Ovid's much-revered *Metamorphoses*, although there are significant differences in the depiction of the characters in the story, with Shakespeare preferring a Venus who is at one with nature, little more than a wild animal herself and urging Adonis to hunt only harmless animals.

Shakespeare's sonnets are, of course, his most famous poetic endeavours, with 154 of them surviving to this day. They consist of 14 lines, are broken into three quatrains (four lines) and end with a rhyming couplet. This came to be known as the English sonnet or Shakespearean sonnet, distinct from the Italian or Petrarchan sonnet, which instead had an eight-line *octet* and a six-line *sestet*. The English sonnet will set up the problem in the first two quatrains and then a solution in the next quatrain and has a concluding couplet. The Italian sonnet establishes the problem in the first eight lines and then offers a solution in the final six. This shift, or *volta*, offers a way to resolve the argument presented in each. These different approaches to developing and resolving an argument can provide a useful vehicle for considering the structure of the arguments students themselves will produce, reflecting on how different forms may lead to different responses and why the position of a volta, the use of rhetorical questions or adding a concluding point to summarise. These short arguments can help to shape our way of addressing a reader and guiding their responses.

How to teach it

There are a multitude of ways in which we can explore Shakespeare's use of language, but it is unlikely to mean very much to students if they first don't have a sense of plot and overall structure of the text. Much as with poetry, students can often strive for immediate understanding, having spent a great deal of time focusing on decoding and comprehension with other texts. But as with studying poetry, one of the joys of the study of Shakespeare is that you gradually unravel meaning, often returning time and again to see something new. This is something which makes him both enduring and exciting to his readers and audiences. A race to comprehension can be unsatisfying and frustrating, so be clear that it may well take multiple readings and perseverance to allow students to feel confident about his style, language and meaning. I spend time first ensuring an understanding of the basic story using summaries, cold reads and a combination of the two in order to set the scene. I also clarify who the characters are and how they relate to each other, so this is embedded prior to analysis. This can be counter-intuitive when often we will quickly move to asking students to identify meaning, but with careful questioning, prediction and reflection we can ensure students have the foundational knowledge they need.

So, to take a specific example, when I am teaching *Macbeth* I will spend some time tracing the idea of blood. As mentioned elsewhere, the word *blood* and references to it appear throughout the play. It is 'stepp'd in so far'(*Macb.*, III, iv, 137) just as much as Macbeth says he is. I begin by asking students to consider what blood may represent. It can be the 'mad blood stirring' Benvolio talks about in *Romeo and Juliet* (*Rom. & Jul.*, III, i, 4), indicating anger and passion, evoking the concept of the *humours*.[7] It can also be representative of the family line, lineage, as well as manifestations of violence and guilt. The blood on the murderers' hands, Lady Macbeth's indelible mark she can't erase, the blood of the Macduffs which Macbeth's soul is 'too much charg'd' (*Macb.*, V, vii, 34) with at the end of

---

7   The Greek physician Galen, building on the writing of Hippocrates, developed the notion of the *humours*; four bodily fluids linked to physical health. There are four humours: blood, black bile, yellow bile and phlegm. These are held in delicate balance in the body and any loss of equilibrium was thought to lead to physical maladies. This was later linked to mental ailments so, for example, having too much blood in the body could lead to uncontrollable emotions, especially anger – something which physicians rectified by 'bleeding' patients with leeches and suction cups. Equally, too much black bile could lead to a melancholia, as associated with Hamlet. This was a prevalent way of thinking about the human body and mental health, particularly in the Middle Ages, but it was not until advancements in medicine in the 18th century that some of these ideas were fully challenged.

the play and Duncan having 'so much blood' (*Macb.*, V, i, 43) in him, are all key moments in the play. Duncan, being of royal blood, sees his 'silver skin lac'd with his golden blood' (*Macb*, II, iii, 119). When we first hear of Macbeth on the battlefield, the account is that of a blood-soaked scene, where Macbeth's sword is 'smok'd with bloody execution' (*Macb.*, I, ii, 18) and Macbeth ultimately knows 'blood will have blood' (*Macb.*, III, iv, 122). Lady Macbeth calls on the spirits to 'make thick my blood' (*Macb.*, I, v, 44) to give her the courage and cruelty to commit her sin against Duncan and even the potion the witches concoct include blood as two main ingredients; that of the sow and the baboon (*Macb.*, IV, i, 4–45).

Each of these moments can be explored alone, but by considering how blood has become a symbol or motif in the play, we can begin to see more elements of conscious crafting. Shakespeare wanted his audience and his reader to be constantly reminded of the violence, the passion, the murder and the loss of a bloodline throughout the play, once again returning us to anxieties around royal lineage, very much at the fore having reached the end of one royal line with Elizabeth's demise. Each moment is of course closely linked to key contextual points, and we consider the implications for his audience as well as our modern readings of this.

English teacher Matthew Lynch also spends time tracing motifs through language, as outlined in his case study here:

When I introduce the idea of motif in literature, I use a sewing analogy with an illustration, like so:

I explain to students that the author wields the needle and the various threads are themes or big ideas the author weaves into the fabric of their text, whereas a motif is the visible stitching of a thread that keeps surfacing; a recurrent symbol or use of imagery which serves to contribute to a text's overarching theme.

For me, the appeal of teaching motifs is two-fold: primarily they are, by definition, a distinctive recurring idea, symbol, concept or structural feature, meaning the *pattern* is one which younger readers of Shakespeare can quite easily identify. Secondly, because they can be more readily identified, they are traceable – thus helping students to navigate a complex text, enabling them to better understand the play's central concerns or big ideas. Two fascinating motifs in *Macbeth* are the motif of birds and the motif of hands, both of which I have recorded presentations on as part of Litdrive's free online CPD (continuing professional development) programme.[8] So, how might we track a motif across a literature text? I have previously used a simple table with success, like the ones below:

Tracking the bird motif in Shakespeare's *Macbeth*				
Act/Scene	Type of bird	Quotation	Character(s) associated with this bird	Significance of the bird as a symbol/imagery

Tracking the hands motif in Shakespeare's *Macbeth*				
Act/Scene	Reference to hand	Quotation	Character or moment associated with hands	Significance of the hands as a symbol/imagery

---

8   Matthew Lynch, 'Macbeth: The Motif of Birds', *Litdrive* (7 November 2020). Available at: https://litdrive.org.uk/remotecpd/m-lynch-macbeth-motif-of-birds.

As we read the play, students will continue to filter relevant textual details onto the tracker resource like the ones above. Doing so provides opportunities for reflection, discussion and for explicit instruction of any historical, cultural contextual information where this might be required. With the motif-of-hands tracker, I invite students also to colour-code each of the three themes to which individual quotations relate, so that they can also develop an appreciation of how ideas in the play are structured – from initial ideas about loyalty and disloyalty through to ideas of guilt and moving towards justice. This serves to support students' understanding of historical contextual information, such as the Great Chain of Being disrupted by Macbeth's act of regicide, the terrible guilt both he and, later, Lady Macbeth experience, and the way in which social order is ultimately restored in the denouement.

Having completed the tracker as part of their study of, and reflections on, the play, time needs then to be given over for students to evaluate which references are most crucial to the development of the theme; perhaps six or eight key motif references spanning the text. Jennifer Webb, in her book *How to Teach English Literature*, refers to textual details like these as 'Swiss army knife quotations'.[9] The amount of support and modelling required here will be informed by the ability of the students whom you are teaching. With students of all abilities, for example, I invite them to select quotations which relate to pivotal moments in the text, but with more able students I might also encourage them to try linking pairs of quotations – perhaps to demonstrate the development of a character or to highlight an interesting juxtaposition, or even a contrast between two characters. By way of illustration, I might model this pair of quotations, drawing students' attention to the subtle juxtaposition of 'head and hand' in the former with 'heart and hand' in the latter: Macbeth admits, 'Strange things I have in head that will to hand / That must be acted 'ere they be scanned' (III, iv, 139–140). Despite his desire to act without thought, here Macbeth acknowledges that he is carefully scheming and rationally plotting his next move, using his 'head' – a symbol of rational thought – to inform his 'hand' – a symbol of thought translated into action. I then juxtapose this with a later

---

9   Jennifer Webb, *How to Teach English Literature: Overcoming Cultural Poverty* (Woodbridge: John Catt Educational, 2019), p. 58.

quotation to demonstrate the subtle shift in Macbeth's psychology, demonstrating that Macbeth later acts impulsively and irrationally, recklessly submitting to emotion or instinct to guide his hand, now acting without thinking: 'From this moment on / The very firstlings of my heart shall be the firstlings of my hand' (*Macb.*, IV, i, 147–148).

Likewise, tracking Shakespeare's recurrent use of bird symbolism in *Macbeth* can serve, amongst other things, to aid students' understanding of the concept of Macbeth as tragic hero. Macbeth is first depicted as an eagle; a bird associated with fierce nobility, grace and piety. As the drama unfolds, he swiftly becomes the nocturnal owl – a bird detested by Jacobeans and one closely associated with death, behaving unnaturally as he 'hawk'd at and killed' (*Macb.*, II, iv, 13) Duncan (the majestic, diurnal falcon), while later still Macbeth is described as a despicable 'hell-kite' (*Macb.*, IV, iii, 217). In this way, by tracking the motif of birds and the way Shakespeare consciously crafts his language to foreground this change in Macbeth's character, students are later able to articulate their understanding of Shakespeare's depiction of Macbeth as a tragic hero more organically, cultivating a more mature, sensitive appreciation of the text and synthesising conceptual ideas more organically in their responses rather than social, cultural and historical contexts or concepts being 'bolted on' arbitrarily, offering nothing meaningful to the students' otherwise personal, critical response.

As Matt demonstrates, tracing motifs and symbols is not only a powerful way to get students to engage with the language of the writer, but also an opportunity to examine how context shapes the choices the writer makes. Patterns in the text can reveal a lot about the ideas which Shakespeare is presenting, as well as how he is shaping the responses of the audience as the play progresses.

Applying it to the classroom

+ Begin by giving students an overview of the plot, characters and themes. Good quality performance, coupled with summary and questioning, will mean students arrive at language analysis ready to see how it relates to these bigger ideas. Audio readings of the plays can also be useful here to allow them to hear the language spoken and to model fluency.

+ Reassure students they won't *get* it all immediately. Explain that the joy in studying Shakespeare's language comes from the gradual understanding we gain and how it enriches our understanding, which is a process: one which even those familiar with his work will continue to go through. It is a process where we layer understanding, deepening each time we revisit it. If students have been used to exploring simpler texts this might be a challenge at first to consider this different approach, but model this for them, demonstrating how you can return to the same quote or extract again and again to delve deeper each time.

+ Look at short extracts and quotes from across a play or a range of texts to examine patterns and connections. Linger on individual words and then trace them as they are used elsewhere so students can notice where these links are and hypothesise as to why.

+ Use freely available searches like *Open-Source Shakespeare*[10] as a method to explore the frequency and location of key words and phrases. For example, a search reveals there are 41 direct references to 'blood' or 'bloody' in the play *Macbeth*, some of which are clustered within a few lines. This provides an opportunity to explore why this is the case and what Shakespeare was doing with these language choices. Equally, looking for references to the sun in *Romeo and Juliet* reveals 17 instances, and if then cross-referenced with light it brings forth a further 34 references, suggesting that there is a motif running through the text which demands further attention. Allowing students to explore this trail in their discussions and consider the prevalence of some words over others can reveal much about the themes Shakespeare was trying to convey too. For example, simply looking at the light and dark references in *Romeo*

---

10 See https://www.opensourceshakespeare.org/.

and Juliet enables students to see the binaries he has woven into the play to mirror the idea of conflict.

* Discuss the imagery Shakespeare is trying to create with his language via pictures, selecting those which are most appropriate to convey his choices at different points. Thinking about how different audiences may respond to these is also a useful way to examine alternative interpretations of a single word, line or idea. This can also support learners with different needs as they have visual images to link to ideas, especially abstract ones, repeated throughout the text. This will provide them with something more concrete to link to the text and, as images are repeated throughout the narrative, can act as support for the working memory and enhance fluency of retrieval as they recognise the recurring images visually. This can be particularly useful for EAL students, supporting them to follow the plot and explore the patterns that emerge.

* Teach aspects of metre (such as iambic and trochaic pentameter), ensuring students have lots of opportunities to hear the language spoken aloud so they can appreciate the musicality of the language and choice of form. Using methods such as *walking the text*, a method whereby students physically walk around the room whilst reading the text and responding to the punctuation, can be a powerful way to convey how a character feels at any given point. Lots of phrases, short clauses, or single syllable words can change the pace of the reading and we should model this and give students the opportunity to examine how this may then impact on performance. Long, languid sentences can create a different performance, and where the punctuation has finally landed in his work can reveal a lot about how a character or scene has been read. Try different ways of reading a single line to illustrate why we place emphasis on certain words and pauses at different points.

* As well as modelling reading for students, employing practices such as choral reading (where the class all read the text aloud together with you) or echo reading (where they repeat lines back) can be another way in which we remove the barriers the language can create. Students build confidence over time as the language becomes more familiar but also they do not feel so exposed as they are reading with the group, and not alone.

* Let students play with and manipulate the language so they are familiar with it, and it doesn't become a block to their interaction

with the plays. Pre-teach the vocabulary, letting students consider words in isolation and explore quotes so that they don't become overwhelmed at trying to interpret them. Even translating short phrases and passages can provide a useful coding activity which can support later analysis.

Chapter 6

Bringing Forth His Theatre

Performance, Stagecraft and Audience

All the world's a stage,

And all the men and women merely players

(AYL, II, vii, 139)

Why teach it?

I think it is first fair to say that Shakespeare was likely to be fixated on the idea of performance, stagecraft and audience. References to acting, performance and *players* make frequent appearances in his writing, with the idea of how we are all performers in the great show of life discussed in both *As You Like It* in the quote at the start of the chapter, and *Macbeth* where he muses on the insignificance of our role, our strutting ultimately 'signifying nothing' (V, v, 28). Equally players, plays within plays and performance are frequently deployed in his works, with appearances in *Hamlet*, *A Midsummer Night's Dream* and *The Taming of the Shrew*. He breaks the *fourth wall* well before Brecht had popularised the notion and often explores the idea of costume, disguise and identity in both comedies and tragedies alike.[1] There is humour in his take on this and the players are often comedic, offering respite even in the most

---

1   The idea of the fourth wall is where characters directly address the audience in some way, moving beyond the realms of the stage to bring them into the action. This was done especially well in the recent National Theatre production of *Julius Caesar* where the staging drew the audience in, casting them as the citizens as performers danced with them and blurred the lines between audience and performer. More traditionally this is done as actors acknowledge the artifice of the play; for example, referencing the fact they are in a play – something Shakespeare does at the end of *A Midsummer Night's Dream* – or where soliloquys are addressed directly to the audience in a conscious way. The same can be said of asides and much can be made of how and when he deploys these devices.

tragic of plays. However, he also uses this as a medium by which to explore some of the biggest questions around humanity, such as what part we play and our significance in the world, and he was working predominantly in a form which would be seen on the stage by a huge proportion of his audience. He himself was a *player* as well as a writer, and experienced his plays from many different perspectives, with suggestions that he first played the young Hamlet in his youth, but later the ghost of Hamlet as he aged. Revision is part of performance and different versions of the plays, adapted for his stage as well as later incarnations, are important considerations in considering how we read his work.

What is it?

This sounds like a rather odd question when discussing play scripts, but considering aspects of stagecraft and performance in Shakespeare is complex. First, there are the contextual points around performance in the Elizabethan era; understanding how the nature of performance, both in terms of tradition and in terms of limitations of the staging, can provide an interesting element for students to explore, especially as we ask them to step away from the cinematic world they are used to. Staging of these plays is different in different contexts and we should let students examine these. Film can be an important way in which we can introduce the students to the plays, and there are many excellent productions to draw on. The use of music, costume, lighting and other elements of cinematography can enliven many readings of the plays which more traditional staging may not provide. The collective sigh when Romeo is pictured on a ruined stage to the strains of Thom Yorke in Baz Luhrmann's *William Shakespeare's Romeo + Juliet*[2] was always a wonderful classroom moment, as was their response as Mercutio leapt onto the scene miming to Candi Staton's *Young Hearts Run Free*. The unfamiliar language seems to take second place to the thrilling and exciting images and sounds on the screen and provides a perfect bridge to what is to follow.

All performance and adaptation, though, have significant elements of interpretation embedded in them. If you were to look at six different productions of the same play, you will find significant differences in

---

2   *William Shakespeare's Romeo + Juliet*, dir. Baz Luhrmann (1996).

terms of how these are being performed, influenced by directorial choices and the delivery and presentation of the actors. This is often something which students don't necessarily consider, which is why it can be powerful to examine different approaches to the same scenes – for example, the opening of *Macbeth* – with some breathtaking interpretations available. As we look at performance, we carefully deconstruct some of the directorial choices to consider how they relate to the text. Even simply looking at costume choices and casting can provide interesting new directions to explore when we return to the text. Experiencing the text as performance is completely different to approaching it as they would a novel, and if we are to add student performance too, further nuance can be found; I have been lucky to have seen some subtle and thoughtful presentations of characters through a student's delivery of a soliloquy. As we discuss and explore their performance choices, layers of understanding around characters and theme can be revealed.

There are also some significant differences to consider in terms of the work as a script. Unlike writers like J. B. Priestley or Arthur Miller, stage directions are sparse, which means there needs to be other methods whereby actors knew how to present the ideas within. The dialogue and language therefore become central to performance, with nuances in delivery capable of shifting meaning and focus significantly. Just experiment with looking at the different performances of Act I, sc. v in *Macbeth* where Lady Macbeth seeks to convince her husband to kill his king. Even subtle difference in position, intonation and emphasis can shift how we see their relationship at this point considerably. I have done work with a group from the Royal Shakespeare Company (RSC) looking at the conflict between Juliet and her father (*Macb.*, III, v, 147–197) and similarly, the same lines can be used in a myriad of ways. Understanding the wider context of the words within and beyond the play can support many different readings, as noted with Katherina's speech in *The Taming of the Shrew* earlier (see page 77). Equally, working with his punctuation (another activity I have undertaken with the RSC) can reveal elements of performance which other writers may have included in direction. Short broken lines may be indicative of internal conflicts which are only partly conveyed by the words alone and seeing these in performance can emphasise many different ideas.

How to teach it

Just as with historical and critical readings of the text, performance and adaptation involves revision of the texts. This is something that should be considered carefully when we think about the performances we introduce to students or ask them to engage with in performance. One approach that has been popular in embedding key points about plot and character has been the *whoosh* version of the plays. This combines storytelling, with students acting out key moments in the play. It is high energy and engaging for students, especially in primary schools, but this has been an approach I've seen used in Year 7 for both *The Tempest* and *Twelfth Night*. The teacher narrates key plot points to set the scene and link the moments. There are lots of other ways we can start to embed an understanding of plot and character, but if we want an exciting and fast-paced way into the play and want to begin with students in performance, this can be a good approach. Following this with carefully layered reminders over the sequence of learning, means students will be able to recall how they and their peers enacted different elements of the story and hang the most salient plot points onto it.

Teaching Shakespeare to younger students, or those whose literacy is still developing, brings a new set of challenges, where students will find the language even more of a barrier in the first instance. Often extracts are used to allow students to engage with his ideas, with the famous 'Seven Ages of Man' speech from *As You Like It* a popular staple in primary settings (II, vii, 140–166). Whilst the use of adaptations and performance can be particularly important for younger children to be able to engage with the complexity of his ideas, concerns about perceived difficulties should not in itself be a barrier to introducing his work at this phase. There are, again, a lot of opportunities to use his language to develop vocabulary of younger and older students.

Importantly, Shakespeare can inspire students of all ages, as argues Lekha Sharma, primary specialist and author, in her case study that follows:

No one is born with skills in writing per se. Those skills may not have come from stylebooks, but they must have come from somewhere. That somewhere is the writing of other good writers.

Steven Pinker[3]

In his book *The Process of Education*, Jerome Bruner states, 'We begin with the hypothesis that any subject can be taught effectively in some intellectually honest form to any child at any stage of development.'[4] This notion, for me, holds entirely true and is particularly pertinent in primary education. At a holistic level, the primary phase is concerned with a number of *end goals* but, when I really ponder about this, one of the most important purposes, in my eyes, is to lay sound conceptual foundations that form the basic building blocks for pupils' understanding and knowledge across subjects. Suffice to say, the works of William Shakespeare are indeed a crucial building block in the literary scholar's development and there really is a case for that journey beginning in the primary years. Pupils' understanding of literature and text evolves at a phenomenal pace throughout their time in primary school. In the Early Years and Key Stage 1, pupils develop a foundational understanding and template of conventional *story* which they then go on to embellish and develop over time. Shakespeare is a key facet to this understanding and offers valuable cross-curricular opportunities, which not only develop concept of plot, character and theme but of chronology, continuity and change and historical significance. So how does one go about teaching these seminal works to pupils aged 8–11?

Inspired by Bruner's hypothesis, we must first wholeheartedly accept that the works of Shakespeare can indeed be taught at some intellectually honest level to pupils at any stage of education. It's all in the delivery! Teasing out the key concepts and key driver questions is at the crux of teaching Shakespeare at primary. What is it we are truly trying to unpick and uncover? Are we taking a close look at the historical context utilising a play such as *Julius Caesar*? Or are we delving deeper into characterisation and setting description through

3   Steven Pinker, *The Sense of Style: The Thinking Person's Guide to Writing in the 21st Century* (London: Penguin, 2015), p. 5.
4   Jerome Bruner, *The Process of Education* (New York: Vintage Books, 1960), p. 33.

study of *Macbeth*? Either way, a clear purpose needs to be established around what will need to be known and understood by the end of the unit, and there should be a considered rationale as to why a particular play is chosen.

The Shakespeare Stories by Andrew Matthews and Tony Ross are wonderful retellings of the Bard's best loved plays and provide visually engaging and accessible versions that can be used to begin pupils' exploration of his work.[5] The texts themselves aren't overly challenging but this reduction in complexity of text opens the door to discussion around some of the more challenging concepts that are unearthed along the way.

A unit might begin with the immersion and exploration of a given text with an overarching driver question that is explored upon beginning the unit. The evolution of the responses to this driver question throughout the unit will offer telling insights into the depth of pupils' understanding and can provide an anchor to return to sporadically across this unit, enabling pupils to navigate abstract concepts and ideas confidently. This provides pupils with a great way to refine their thinking and ideas about the plot, characters and storyline over time and will allow them to develop the skill of grappling with the text to draw refined conclusions – a type of *reading resilience* that will most definitely stand them in good stead as they continue to explore English literature and language. At this early stage of exploration, oracy and performance can play a powerful part; these mediums can allow pupils to refine and shape their thinking about the driver question with their peers, allowing what is known as cognitive restructuring to take place. As Robin Alexander so eloquently puts it, 'Language not only manifests thinking but also structures it and speech shapes the higher mental processes necessary for so much of the learning that takes place, or ought to take place in school.'[6]

After pupils have secured their understanding of the storyline and have established a secure knowledge of the characters and plot, you can then dig deeper on a particular extract or part of the text, focusing in on a key writing technique that you may want to explore

5   Andrew Matthews and Tony Ross, *The Shakespeare Stories* (New York: Orchard Books, 2016).
6   Robin Alexander, *Essays on Pedagogy* (Abingdon and New York: Routledge, 2013), p. 92.

further. This might be, for example, exploration of the setting description of the storm that Prospero conjures in *The Tempest*. We may want to explicitly unpick how mood and atmosphere has been created here and endeavour to delineate how Shakespeare went about doing this and how we can add to our *writer's toolkit*. As Steven Pinker puts it in *The Sense of Style*, 'Writers acquire their technique by spotting, savoring and reverse engineering examples of good prose.'[7] Pupils may then go on to construct their own descriptions of a storm, embedding the techniques and language from the initial text and drawing from this toolkit to develop their own individual writer's style and a bespoke amalgamation of their ever-growing mental library of literary techniques and styles they have been exposed to throughout their learning journey. And so why shouldn't we expose our primary pupils to the greats such as Shakespeare? May it light a fire in their bellies and lay the foundations for their lifelong journey of literature.

I can see no better reason to teach Shakespeare, or any other quality text or knowledge, than to 'light a fire in their bellies' – and many, many schools are doing this in different ways. Sarah Harris, also a primary specialist working at Redwell Primary in Northamptonshire, and an English lead, not only utilises the power of performance with her students, but the power of storytelling too:

Storytelling techniques are at the heart of our school curriculum with an emphasis on creating storytellers, readers and authors, so, naturally, we have used many of the key strategies and principles of storytelling to support our children's exploration and enjoyment of Shakespeare. Having taught Shakespeare as an extracurricular club in primary for several years, I saw first-hand the power of Shakespeare through practical application shine through Years 3–6. Moving schools allowed me to plan key plays into each Key Stage 2 classroom through their English curriculum, but how have we engaged, excited and deepened the children's understanding?

---

7   Pinker, *The Sense of Style*, p. 5.

To begin the unit, we wanted to ignite the children's curiosity. This started by utilising drama techniques such as Object In The Bag: a miniature ship, a magic book and a staff allowed the children to first consider how these objects were connected and create improvisations as a basis for their predictions of the story they were linked to. The children were immediately engaged and enthused, with many asking questions and pulling in connections from texts explored over the year. Further piquing their interests, we shared a mixed-up storyboard to give another layer of understanding. In order to boost their oxygen levels and increase their collaborative talk, we placed the mixed-up pictures around the classroom and asked them to go and stand by the one they were most interested in. The children then discussed some of the finer details of that part of the story and built upon each other's ideas. Continued movement allowed the children to stand by the one they were least excited by, the one they thought was the beginning of the story and the one they believed to be the ending. This unobtrusive activity allowed for them to be discussing key details of the story and build in ideas whilst not feeling overwhelmed by some of the complexities of language.

Our next step was to launch our story through storytelling techniques. Being a Storytelling School, most of our units start with the adult becoming a storyteller and the children getting lost in an imaginative world.[8] Key strategies within this include audience participation, so, in my initial telling of *The Tempest*, the children created the soundscape of the storm, mimicked key actions for key characters and gradually started to echo back some carefully chosen lines for the play. Key parts of the story were repeated throughout with gaps utilised to increase the children's retrieval. For example, as the story went on, I would start a key line and then encourage the children to complete it. Weeks since the launch of the story and I can still hear children declare they are Prospero whilst rolling their tongues for emphasis and holding a powerful stance. Minimal resources are needed for storytelling, but I can't help but use instruments sometimes; cue a triangle played every time Ariel entered the story. These simple character cues, whether it be a key word or line, a powerful stance or action or a musical signal, acted like a signpost

---

8   Storytelling School is an approach to learning focusing on oracy and presentation. More details about the specific approach can be found here: https://storytellingschools.com/.

to their memory and allowed them to keep recalling in confidence the key character's name and their role in the story.

In our initial response discussions, through the use of Aidan Chambers' *Book Talk* prompts, it was evident that the children loved the ending and the powerful Prospero but were finding it difficult to keep track of all the characters.[9] Again, it was storytelling techniques and drama strategies that we used to deepen their understanding further: Rolling Theatre (based on an approach where drama is used as a medium for the teaching of English, as explored in the *Developing Drama in English* handbook in 2010[10]), miming scenes and thought-tapping all played a part. They would not be seeing a written version of the story until they felt confident in the key stepping stones and themes within the story. Some of you may wonder why we do this but, for me, the removal of a written text, for now, eliminates some of the daunting barriers that primary children have felt when they first set their eyes on a Shakespearean text. The barrier of knowing what the words mean are temporarily removed, which means when they are faced with the written version of the text, they already have a good level of understanding and confidence in approaching it. Primary children need to explore high-quality and complex texts; a practical approach which removes the phonetic barriers and fear of complex language allows them to explore, through the feeling of the text, the joyous sound of the language and to become the key characters in order to develop their depth of understanding, even at the level of Shakespeare.

The storytelling elements here, along with the use of actions and gestures, ensured that students were able to access the joy of the narrative and had a doorway into the text which didn't require them first to navigate the language. Oracy is central to all we do with our students, and traditions of oral storytelling have long allowed the transference of knowledge across the generations. Here Sarah creates a perfect blend of this to enable students to explore the work of Shakespeare in a meaningful way.

---

9   Aidan Chambers, *Book Talk: Occasional Writing on Literature and Children* (Woodchester: Thimble Press, 1995).

10 Department for Education, *Developing Drama in English: A Handbook for English Subject Leaders and Teachers* (2010). Available at: https://dera.ioe.ac.uk/779/7/431361fb6069ab0e0b57b230e8ab5aab_Redacted.pdf.

Adaptation, performance and focusing on the narrative aspects of the plays do not only have a place in primary schools. Exploring different interpretations, either through comparison of performance or engaging actively with their own performances, is a useful way to develop an appreciation of Shakespeare's work and I am yet to see two performances that emphasise the same points, even where the directorial choices are more traditional. Being able to evaluate different interpretations and build new understanding around this is a rich seam to mine. Workshops run by drama companies, including those run by the RSC, have been useful in developing my own understanding of his texts, with things such as walking the punctuation in Act I, sc. vii of *Macbeth* providing another way to model different readings to a class, and directorial choices creating new resonance as mentioned. The constant onstage presence of the Porter in the 2018 Globe production mentioned earlier, or with the difference between Katherina placing her hand beneath that of her husband at the end of *The Taming of the Shrew* or having him kneel before her at the end of the production, as highlighted by Emma Smith in her excellent lecture on the play from the Oxford University *Approaching Shakespeare* podcast series, makes a significant difference to our whole reading of the play.[11] Whilst I do not believe that Shakespeare can only be understood through performance, and there is much to be gained through a close analysis of his language and structures, exploring aspects of doubling through performance and adaptation can be powerful. For example, the use of the same actors to play seemingly different roles can really emphasise Shakespeare's obsession with doubles, and doubling, such as in the National Theatre's 2020 production of *A Midsummer Night's Dream*, directed by Nicholas Hytner.[12] Gwendoline Christie and Oliver Chris, cast as both Hippolyta and Titania and Theseus and Oberon, brought a new dynamic to the couples, emphasising the gender power struggles in a play whose language is filled with parallels, echoes and inversions. By exposing students to a range of different performances and giving them the opportunities to debate, discuss and examine these choices themselves can deepen their understanding. Equally, examining different receptions to the play can help them to reconsider authorial intent and the significance of Shakespeare through the ages.

---

11 Emma Smith, 'Taming of the Shrew', *Approaching Shakespeare* [podcast]. Available at: https://podcasts.ox.ac.uk/taming-shrew-0.
12 *A Midsummer Night's Dream*, dir. Nicholas Hytner [play] (National Theatre, 2018).

Applying it to the classroom

+ Make use of different performances, drawing comparisons focusing on interpretation. This is especially successful when looking at the delivery and performance of key scenes. Watching two different openings to a play can support students to think critically and move away from the idea there is only one performance or interpretation we can use. This leads us to greater originality in interpretation and reinforces the idea that these plays are constructs which change over the course of time.

+ Consider how different settings, direction, intonation and body language can convey different aspects of meaning. For example, focusing on whether Katherina, at the end of *The Taming of the Shrew*, yields to her husband's kiss willingly and how these two characters position themselves can reveal a lot of different ways to read the final scene. Equally, the position and movement of silent characters at a key moment, such as Hippolyta at the start of *A Midsummer Night's Dream*, whose body language will immediately shape how we will read the relationship between her and her new husband, can again reveal a great deal about the character and the power relations at this point. Model this for students so they can see how this may change our understanding.

+ Allow students to explore how they might dramatise an extract, everything from the reading of single words and lines to whole scenes. This is something that can work well with exchanges between Macbeth and Lady Macbeth as they discuss the murder of the King, or as Benedict and Beatrice explore their feelings for each other.

+ Make use of links with theatre companies such as the Royal Shakespeare Company and The Globe, who have educational programmes and performances which are suitable for a range of age groups and disciplines. This includes visits to schools and online options for further geographical reach.

+ Reflect on the props that different plays might need. Some props in plays like *The Comedy of Errors*, *Macbeth* or *The Merchant of Venice* take on a symbolic meaning (for example, the chain representing the connection between characters, the crown and the three caskets) and can again enrich understanding.

+ Examine differences between playscripts, adding and removing stage directions or going through the process of directing others to consider where the clues are in the language and structure.

+ Performance can be especially useful for EAL learners or those with some special educational needs. The fact they can still engage with the action, just as other students will be doing, can provide an opening to the text. If you are using performance with a group with a range of needs, sticking to a core performance will help them, as will using images from the same performance when you are using images to reinforce who is speaking or the specific point in the text.

Chapter 7

Bringing Forth His Influence

Intertextuality and Reach

There Shakespeare, on whose forehead climb
The crowns o' the world; O eyes sublime
With tears and laughter for all time!

Elizabeth Barrett Browning, *A Vision of Poets*[1]

Why teach it?

As I said at the start of this book, like him or loathe him, Shakespeare's reach has been wide. His influence cannot only be found in works of literature, but also in our artwork and our music, with paintings such as those by John Everett, whose image of Ophelia provides a haunting image familiar to many, and Brahms' *Ophelia-Lieder*, moving operagoers to tears. *The Shakespere Allusion Book: A Collection of Allusions to Shakespere from 1591–1700* collates a huge number of allusions others made to his work, suggesting that his work as collaborator, influencer and inspirer existed not only in our modern imaginations but in the world in which he lived.[2] However, whilst we can always argue that there may be better playwrights, better poets and potentially better uses of our curriculum time, to not spend some time studying Shakespeare's work would risk removing our students from the discussions around his importance and having the opportunity to see just how far the threads of his influence weave into the tapestry of our society. We are always

---

1 Elizabeth Barrett Browning, 'A Vision of Poets'. In *Elizabeth Barrett Browning's Poetical Works Vol. I* [ebook] (Project Gutenberg, 2011 [1890]). Available at: https://www.gutenberg.org/files/37452/37452-h/37452-h.htm.
2 John Munro (ed.), *The Shakespere Allusion Book: A Collection of Allusions to Shakespere from 1591–1700*, originally compiled by Clement Mansfield Ingleby, Lucy Toulmin Smith and Frederick J. Furnivall (London: Chatto & Windus, 2007 [1909]).

gatekeepers of our curriculum and every selection we make, both to include or remove, needs careful consideration. Modern writers and filmmakers still take his work as an inspiration, with anything from *Westside Story*, *Ten Things I Hate About You*, *Throne of Blood* and the less impressive *She's the Man*, taking its inspiration from the cross-dressing delights of *Twelfth Night*, all drawing directly from his work. Songwriters and musicians too continue to draw on his ideas, with everyone from Taylor Swift to Iron Maiden calling upon his ideas to illustrate their work. However, it is not only the direct adaptations and references which we can explore, but also how far he has influenced our understanding of the world. Nelson Mandela, who kept a copy of Shakespeare's complete works by his bed whilst incarcerated, said, 'Shakespeare always seems to have something to say to us' and Ben Jonson declared him as a man 'not of an age, but for all time'.[3]

One of the things students often complain about is the relevance of his work to their lives. By examining the intertextuality, modern interpretation – especially through performance and textual reimagining – such as we see with Margaret Atwood's *Hag-Seed* or Tracey Chevalier's *New Boy*, students can begin to see what value he may, or may not, hold for them.[4] Some teachers talk about the *hook* which will draw their students in, and seeing *Romeo and Juliet* sit alongside discussions around gang and knife crime, parent–child relationships and the intoxicating power of adolescent love can indeed provide a medium through which students can explore important ideas. Equally, looking at consequences in the world of *Macbeth* and considering the topic of morality and what you are prepared to do for fame/money/power are concerns which link us to both modern popular celebrity and politics, some of which seem now to overlap. The National Theatre production of *Julius Caesar* used this to interesting effect, with Caesar arriving on the stage to rapturous applause and what appeared to be a red baseball cap, signifying some interesting links to modern America at the time of production.[5]

3   Robert McCrum, 'Ten ways in which Shakespeare changed the world', *The Guardian* (17 April 2016). Available at: https://www.theguardian.com/culture/2016/apr/17/ten-ways-shakespeare-changed-the-world.
4   Margaret Atwood, *Hag-Seed* (London: Hogarth, 2016); Tracey Chevalier, *New Boy* (London: Vintage Press, 2018).
5   *Julius Caesar*, dir. Tony Grech-Smith and Nicholas Hytner [play] (National Theatre, 2018).

What is it?

Intertextuality is looking at the dialogue which takes place between different texts and writers. It is about moving away from looking at plays and ideas in isolation, although these have much merit, and looking at how writers write back or relate to the original work. One example of this in the world of Shakespeare is considering his contemporaries, with John Fletcher, a collaborator of Shakespeare's, actually writing a sequel to *The Taming of the Shrew*. Characters which Shakespeare was bringing to life in his productions were equally present in the writing of Christopher Marlowe and George Chapman and he was not by far the only person writing for the stage in this era.

However, just as with using different critical lenses to shape our interpretation, exploring intertextuality can enrich our understanding of his work as well as challenge our interpretation of it and the ideas it contains. As with the aforementioned examples from Margaret Atwood – a novel from a series of texts looking at characters from Shakespeare in a different light; a project commissioned by Random House as part of its Hogarth Shakespeare Series – modern interactions with the plays enliven them.[6] Just as it is difficult to read Brontë's *Jane Eyre* now without considering Rhys's Antoinette as the poor creature haunting Rochester's attic once you have encountered *Wide Sargasso Sea*, modern retellings, performances and dialogues with Shakespeare's texts continue to create new meaning.[7] *Shylock Is My Name*, also in the Hogarth Shakespeare Series, takes a much-loathed character and reconsiders his perspective.[8] Tom Stoppard's *Rosencrantz and Guildenstern Are Dead* forever elevates these minor characters into the limelight.[9] We are, I am sure, long due a major retelling of *A Midsummer Night's Dream* from the perspective of Puck or Cobweb as an alternative view of the kingdom.

But if we take a play such as *Romeo and Juliet*, we will often find much of its plot has become part of our collective consciousness, as with his language, as shown in Chapter 5. Two warring families. Two

---

6   The Hogarth Shakespeare Series of books asked modern authors to explore the plays as novels. The series includes not only *Hag-Seed*, but Tracey Chevalier's *New Boy* – a retelling of *Othello* in the playground – and Jeanette Winterson's *A Winter's Tale*. The series can be found here: https://www.penguinrandomhouse.com/series/HSR/hogarth-shakespeare.

7   Jean Rhys, *Wide Sargasso Sea* (London: Penguin Classics, 2000).

8   Howard Jacobson, *Shylock Is My Name* (London: Penguin Random House, 2016).

9   Tom Stoppard, *Rosencrantz and Guildenstern are Dead* (London: Faber & Faber, 1973).

star-crossed lovers who take their lives. Doomed love and images of balcony scenes have been woven into the fabric of our worlds and we all understand what we mean when we refer to those characters and their situations. Many authors have taken direct inspiration from his work, writing their own versions of age-old tales for a different audience or a different form. Equally, many writers have drawn inspiration for their titles, although the work itself doesn't necessarily reflect the content. This is again exploring how their audience may respond to their knowledge of these well-known works, with Aldous Huxley's *Brave New World*, whose title is taken from *The Tempest*, and Ray Bradbury's *Something Wicked This Way Comes* building audience expectations through their use of well-known phrases from Shakespeare to shape audience expectations.[10] Angela Carter's *Wise Children* makes almost continual references to Shakespeare's works, alluding to 26 of his plays and his sonnets too.[11] Carter is a very crafted and conscious writer who is able to draw on a vast array of influences, but her playful use of Shakespeare's plots, quotes and characters in this novel are accompanied by the idea of Shakespeare as *high culture* and makes for an interesting discussion amongst A level students who will also be exploring his plays.

Shakespeare has also influenced our language and there are several words attributed to him as being the first time in known usage, such as *equivocal, prodigious* and *antipathy*.[12] That is in addition to the phrases we no longer even associate with him, which have become part of our everyday language, such as 'fool's gold' (see page 127 for further examples).

How to teach it

Beginning a unit by using a brief version or extract from a modern interpretation can be useful in allowing students to access characters and themes before encountering the language. Bali Rai's *Rani and Sukh* reimagines Romeo and Juliet as young urban British Asians, and Malorie Blackman's *Chasing the Stars* is an effective retelling of *Othello* for an adolescent reader.[13] These will both offer a good grounding in the

---

10 Aldous Huxley, *Brave New World* (London: Penguin Vintage Classics, 2007); Ray Bradbury, *Something Wicked This Ways Comes* (London: Gollancz, 2015).

11 Angela Carter, *Wise Children* (London: Penguin Vintage Classics, 1992).

12 McCrum, 'Ten ways in which Shakespeare changed the world'.

13 Bali Rai, *Rani and Sukh* (London: Corgi, 2004); Malorie Blackman, *Chasing the Stars* (London: Penguin, 2017).

plot and character, but equally will open up the discussion as to why authors may choose to retell these works in a modern world.

Tracing his influence in other texts – for example, looking at where some of the key themes and ideas are revisited – can be a powerful way to build schemas which will lead to longer-term learning and a powerful dialogue around what it is that different writers want to achieve; so, for example, looking at how he explores deception in his plays and where we can see this idea explored again later, in the form of disguise or duplicity.

Equally, examining where some of our frequently used idioms – some of which, even if not of Shakespeare's own creation, certainly linger in our dialect due to the popularity of his work – are an interesting element to explore and again considering how and why these were used, and continue to be, is a way in which we can immerse students into a world of exploration of words and phrases. Here are some of the most common phrases and words which seem to have originated or been popularised by Shakespeare:

- ✦ 'All that glisters isn't gold' (*The Merchant of Venice*)
- ✦ 'As good luck would have it' (*The Merry Wives of Windsor*)
- ✦ 'Break the ice' (*The Taming of the Shrew*)
- ✦ 'Cold comfort' (*King John*)
- ✦ 'Come what come may' (come what may) (*Macbeth*)
- ✦ 'Devil incarnate' (*Titus Andronicus*)
- ✦ 'Eaten me out of house and home' (*2 Henry IV*)
- ✦ 'Fair play' (*The Tempest*)
- ✦ 'A laughing-stock' (*The Merry Wives of Windsor*)
- ✦ 'In a pickle' (*The Tempest*)
- ✦ 'Wear one's heart on one's sleeve' (*Othello*)

Presenting students with these phrases and exploring when and where they may have come across them in everyday usage, even in film and television, is a good starting point for them to see the influence Shakespeare has had on shaping what we say, and even what we may think. This again is a way to demystify his words and show them the connection they already have with his work.

The same is true if you explore some of his insults with students, getting them to play with his use of insult. He was especially good in his comedies at getting characters to throw insults at each other and the scene where Hermia and Helena engage in verbal fisticuffs in *A Midsummer Night's Dream* or the put-downs deployed by Benedict and Beatrice in *Much Ado About Nothing* are often of interest to the students.

For younger students, a Shakespeare Insult Kit, available in multiple forms online, is a good way to get them to play with his language and again see how his language works. Its use in lessons was often followed by the sound of the wordplay bouncing around the corridors at a later time.

One example of such a kit can be seen below:

To create a Shakespearean insult that will really sting, combine one word from each column and preface with the word 'Thou':

Column One	Column Two	Column Three
artless	base-court	baggage
churlish	hedge-born	bugbear
dankish	dog-hearted	luggage mugger
jarring	fly-bitten	maggot-pie
paunchy	folly-fallen	coxcomb
puking	paunchy	varlet
bawdy	beetle-headed	flapdragon
moonface	fool-born	hagseed
weedy	urchin-faced	lout

Exploring his insults in this way not only means that if you select some which will appear in later texts they will recognise them in context, but there are also opportunities to build vocabulary and provide opportunities for pre-teaching as you consider how they might be used in context, examining what is being conveyed in the language by a character. Importantly, students can consider what has become part of our language beyond the bounds of Shakespeare, and when and where they may continue to appear in the range of texts we study elsewhere, thus continuing to cement his influence in the world.

Whilst there are opportunities to explore how Shakespeare's influence has directly inspired our writing, our art, our music and our language, it is not always possible to ascertain exactly how far his influence really does extend. If we take Harold Bloom's argument, Shakespeare has been instrumental in how we think about the very fabric of who we are, entering the discourse of philosophers, religion and psychology.[14] Whilst there are many who will continue to debate what they consider the overemphasis on one man, as shown at the start of this book and in this chapter, his impact can be felt far and wide. Again, this is why it is important that we allow our students to engage with the power of his work, for them to consider the place he may have in their lives and the lives of our future generations.

Helen Ralston, principal of The Rise School in Middlesex, a specialist provision for 4–19-year-olds, explains here how they ensure that the young people they work with are given the opportunity to appreciate Shakespeare's influence, regardless of the issues they may face. She uses an eight-step approach to ensure that all can access and explore his world and enter those conversations across our society.

At The Rise School, we (humbly!) model our provision as being the best of both worlds of mainstream and special education. We imagine our students at 25, 30 or 50 years of age and want them to be able to say 'me too' in those conversations about what you studied at school. Echoing the increased challenge that has been embedded in English department curricula across the country, our students study four full Shakespeare plays between Years 7 and 11.

---

14 Bloom, *Shakespeare*.

When teaching Shakespeare, I start from one simple principle: you cannot enjoy, let alone analyse, what you don't understand. Therefore, the focus of this case study is how I foreground understanding when tackling a full Shakespearean text. The eight ideas that follow were used with my Year 7 class in spring term 2021, much of which was delivered virtually.

Before teaching

We dedicate a whole term to Shakespeare but, having 40-minute lessons, time is still tight. My first step is to (1) ask myself this question: what are the key scenes, moments and speeches that capture the essence of the play – the ones you absolutely cannot miss? In addition to sorting them into a weekly coverage document, I also (2) plot them onto Freytag's plot pyramid.[15] I use two colours to distinguish between the stories of the two main couples. This pyramid will be displayed on a large scale at the front of the room, but equally it can be printed as a sort of placemat. It is referred to at the start of most lessons (see (4) on page 131).

At the start of the teaching sequence

Shakespeare is challenging. Therefore, my first lesson acknowledges this and frames it positively. We look at why Shakespeare has endured, its merit and explore that struggle is healthy and essential to the learning process.

With most texts, I vehemently resist spoilers. Not so with Shakespeare. When you consider the principles of cognitive load and how much our working memory can manage, it's quite clear that the complexity of Shakespeare's language needs to be tackled upon a foundation of understanding the plot, character and their relationships. Therefore, (3) – pre-teaching these aspects using an abridged version – is essential. I like the Andrew Matthews and Tony Ross editions and deploy the 1993 Kenneth Branagh cinematic gem.[16]

---

15 Freytag's plot pyramid was devised by the 19th-century German playwright, Gustav Freytag. Freytag's Pyramid is a visual representation of dramatic structure outlining the seven key steps in successful storytelling: exposition, inciting incident, rising action, climax, falling action, resolution and denouement or conclusion.

16 Matthews and Ross, *The Shakespeare Stories; Much Ado About Nothing*, dir. Kenneth Branagh [film] (BBC, 1993).

During the teaching sequence

After building this solid foundation, we begin analysis. We progress through each of the key scenes already identified and mapped onto the plot pyramid. We will do lessons on each scene: sometimes in its entirety, sometimes a key exchange or speech. The next four strategies are used throughout these closer reading lessons.

(4) My number-one strategy is the power of anchoring your students before digging deep. Where are we in the play? Who is there? What is their relationship with others in the scene? What are their overall emotions and intentions? We need to activate the relevant prior knowledge gained during (3) to unlock the learning in that lesson. I do this by going back to the plot pyramid and actively moving a sticky note up the display. This simple act is important: it quickly orients students; what came before, what is next? It is also motivating to see themselves progress systematically through the play. We may also rewatch a 2–3-minute clip from Branagh, or even just look at a screenshot of the moments whilst I narrate:

'Last lesson we studied the part where Beatrice was mocking Benedick during the masked ball. Now we're going to study the end of that scene where their friends decide that they would be well suited and to do some match-making.'

---

(5) I use the SparkNotes *No Fear* edition of *Much Ado About Nothing*.[17] It is freely accessible online but as we intend to study most of the play we invest in hard copies. I explicitly teach my students how to *read across* the double-page layout so that they can self-scaffold this process in future lessons. I will use simple *quotation quest* tasks where they must use one side to find a quotation from the other.

(6) I comb the scene for archaic and tier 2 vocabulary. As our lessons are short, I need a quick and efficient way to communicate these

---

17 SparkNotes, *No Fear Shakespeare: Much Ado About Nothing* (New York: SparkNotes, 2004).
    Also available online at: https://www.sparknotes.com/nofear/shakespeare/muchado/.

definitions. I will often just have a simple slide that has a modern sentence with the target word in bold:

* In *sevennight*, I'm going on holiday.

  sevennight (n) =

* Reading whilst in the car makes me feel *queasy*.

  queasy (adj) =

We can discuss this in a matter of minutes.

(7) As part of studying a section, I will often show clips from the Globe production. I embrace that it repeats the plot from Branagh as it provides the opportunity to discuss directorial choices and reminds the students that Shakespeare was a playwright. Enjoying a scene that they have encountered on multiple occasions generates those valuable *I get it, I'm in the club* moments that intrinsic motivation is made of.

Lastly, I provide the same model for analytical writing every time I ask Year 7 to write. I want them to apply their precious working memory to exploring Shakespeare's authorial decisions. The scaffold means they can focus on that rather than the mechanics of gluing their ideas into a fluent paragraph. I am at ease that there is plenty of time to fade this support during Key Stage 3. Ideally, the model is printed off so that it's on their desk, right next to where they are writing, so their attention is split less between needing to look up and down.

Outcomes

The above strategies helped my Year 7s thrive when studying *Much Ado About Nothing*. They learnt about allusion, asides, soliloquies, dramatic irony, honour, chastity and patriarchy and the features of Shakespearean comedy. They produced brilliant analytical paragraphs on a wide number of scenes. Pragmatically, I am confident they are well on their way to being about to nail *Macbeth* at Key Stage 4. But more than this, they enjoyed it. We all did.

Assuming that Shakespeare is for some and not for others can be a way to limit how much people from certain backgrounds or situations can engage in those big conversations. The Rise approach gives a positive reminder that Shakespeare is an option for all.

Applying it to the classroom

+ Look at where his influence is apparent. Think about links between themes, character and plot that have influenced other writers. Malorie Blackman's *Noughts & Crosses*, with her own powerful take on divided lovers, and *The Steep and Thorny Way*, inspired by *Hamlet*, by Cat Winters are good places to explore this reimagining.[18] My students particularly enjoyed looking at Simon Armitage's 'Remains' alongside studying *Macbeth*, where they considered the idea of the 'blood shadow' in relation to the guilt of Macbeth and his wife, as well as exploring the position of a soldier in society beyond the war.[19]

+ Make use of texts that use Shakespeare's plots to prepare students for the greater complexity of his own writing and its performance. Abridged versions can be used as an introduction to the text too.

+ Consider where his language appears elsewhere and reflect on why these writers are drawing on this as an allusion. Even the musical *Hamilton* makes references to Macbeth, commenting on the title character's ambition and ruthless drive to success.

+ Consider what we might take away and use in our own work. Play with incorporating his language in our own writing. This has been especially successful with creative writing tasks, where inspiration can be taken from quotes or phrases and can be woven into our own work, as well as borrowing plot lines and characters to rework.

+ Use his modern relevance as a hook to encourage students to think about how his commentary on the world can relate to our context

---

18 Malorie Blackman, *Noughts & Crosses* (London: Penguin, 2001); Cat Winters, *The Steep and Thorny Way* (New York: Amulet Books, 2016).

19 Simon Armitage, 'Remains'. In *The Not Dead* (Keighley: Pomona Books, 2008), pp. 19–21.

and thereby consider why his work has continued to be seen as important.

» Sally O'Reilly, 'Top ten novels inspired by Shakespeare', *The Guardian* (30 April 2014). Available at: https://www. theguardian.com/books/2014/apr/30/top-10-novels-inspired-shakespeare-herman-melville-patricia-highsmith.

» 'Shakespeare on screen', *Into Film*. Available at: https://www. intofilm.org/films/filmlist/11?gclid= CjwKCAjw7rWKBhAtEiwAJ3CWLEOJcR4pB1LYpdmEaZ-QMyAC6sMJABGtEZ54iA3efkeINDyR3l5uRoCSiMQAvD_BwE.

» Robert McCrum, 'Ten ways in which Shakespeare changed the world', *The Guardian* (17 April 2016). Available at: https:// www.theguardian.com/culture/2016/apr/17/ten-ways-shakespeare-changed-the-world.

Conclusion

Now I have laid bare some of the threads of the Bard's work, the important work begins. It is time to think about how we weave these threads back into our curriculum, our lessons and, most importantly, into our students' learning. How can we provide them with a foundation whereby they can decide how and when Shakespeare will fit into their lives? As you will have seen throughout this book, Shakespeare's work remains as relevant today as ever. It has shaped, and continues to shape, our literature and our thinking, including about some of the biggest questions around our society. In his work he reaches back into our history, nestling deeply within our curriculum when we explore the texts of Homer and Virgil and reaching forwards into the work of contemporary writers and poets. Making these links explicit to your students is the key to helping them to understand his significance as a writer and his ability to craft plays and poems that question, challenge and inspire us all. To take this further we need to take a step back and look at the big picture. Interrogate the role Shakespeare plays in our curriculum and find the links to other works. Identify the big questions you want to explore when studying his writing – for example, what he is saying about gender or power or oppression in different moments and in different plays. Consider where other writers pick up on those threads and interleave them with his work or weave the study of his work back in. Consider which writers challenge him too; decide who is presenting a different perspective on ideas of power, gender and family and explore these alongside his work or as an extension of it.

The national curriculum in England to date states that there should be the study of two of his plays at Key Stage 3, and the study of a play is still essential study for GCSE and A level literature. We need to ensure the opportunities we give our students are the right ones, making sure we select his plays that build on what went before and prepare students for the rigours of later study. The issue of equity is central to how and when we are teaching these so all students can access them and be involved in those bigger conversations he draws upon. The temptation with curriculum design, though, is to cram everything in as quickly as possible, but we need to focus on the most salient points, giving students the foundational knowledge at different stages in their education and an opportunity to consider why we persist in returning to his work across the world and throughout the ages. Deciding then on what to focus on and when will depend on your context, what else has been taught and what you and your team have decided you want to pass on.

The difficulties his texts can present means we need a careful process of breaking down the key knowledge our pupils need, reflection on how that will be best conveyed and in what order, and how we will check it is understood by all. We need to model how we talk and write about his work too, leading students to the kind of disciplinary thinking that should pervade our subject. Preparing the ground carefully through sequencing and pre-learning, and introducing this new information in small steps – linked to big conceptual ideas so it is more likely to adhere – are essential elements of teaching the plays, as is careful sequencing which allows us to retrieve and embed the learning. It is also essential that we model how we think about, talk about and write about his work so students can see those processes we go through as we analyse his work, as well as what the outcome should look like. Drawing upon some of our *best bets* in teaching, as outlined in the work of people such as Professor Robert Coe in his *Great Teaching Toolkit*,[1] to ensure we are giving our students the best opportunities to grasp some of the nuances of Shakespeare's writing is as much an important consideration as deciding where and how the plays may fit into our curriculum. These pedagogical approaches take us from what they need to know into how they are going to apply that knowledge.

Equipping students with the tools to reflect, discuss and debate the relevance of the themes and characters presented within his writing will enable them to make significant decisions in their later life as to how and why these concepts fit into their world and continue the debate as to his place in our canon. It will enrich their language choices and help them to understand some of the issues which surround how we have seen this one writer as so influential. An appreciation of Shakespeare can have a lasting and even transformational impact on the choices they may make much further down the line, just as they may have had for his earliest audiences, and we need to be unashamed about why we are teaching them the powerful texts we do – Shakespeare or otherwise. The cultural

---

1 Rob Coe, C. J. Rauch, Stuart Kime and Dan Singleton, *Great Teaching Toolkit: Evidence Review* (June 2020). Available at: https://assets.website-files.com/5ee28729f7b4a5fa99bef2b3/5ee9f507021911ae35ac6c4d_EBE_GTT_EVIDENCE%20REVIEW_DIGITAL.pdf?utm_referrer=https%3A%2F%2Fwww.greatteaching.com.

capital the study of his work provides goes well beyond the realms of his texts, as I hope you have seen as I have explored the inspirations, allusions and influence of his work. I hope, too, that this book has excited you, challenged you and prompted you to want to explore further how Shakespeare can really enrich the experiences of your students. I also hope it has given you an opportunity to reflect upon and enhance your own subject knowledge and to begin your conversations in your schools around what it is your students need. Combining this with the case studies and applying it to teaching points at the end of each chapter, I also hope means you have some takeaways to explore with your classes, so you can create exciting, thought-provoking and enriching lessons that will take your students beyond the bounds of an exam specification or their years in formal education. But I will leave the final words to *A Midsummer Night's Dream's* Puck, as I take my bow and draw the curtain.

> If we shadows have offended, Think but this, and all is mended, That you have but slumber'd here While these visions did appear. And this weak and idle theme, No more yielding but a dream, Gentles, do not reprehend: If you pardon, we will mend: And, as I am an honest Puck, If we have unearned luck Now to 'scape the serpent's tongue, We will make amends ere long; Else the Puck a liar call: So, good night unto you all. Give me your hands, if we be friends, And Robin shall restore amends.

(*Mids. N D.*, V, ii, 54–69)

Bibliography

Ackroyd, Peter (2006). *Shakespeare: The Biography*. London: Vintage Publishing.

Adelman, Janet (1992). *Suffocating Mothers: Fantasies of Maternal Origin in Shakespeare's Plays, Hamlet to The Tempest*. London: Psychology Press.

Alexander, Robin (2013). *Essays on Pedagogy*. Abingdon and New York: Routledge.

Armitage, Simon (2008). 'Remains'. In *The Not Dead*. Keighley: Pomona Books, pp. 19–21.

Atwood, Margaret (2016). *Hag-Seed*. London: Hogarth.

Bakhtin, Mikhail (2009). *Rabelais and His World*, tr. Helene Iswolsky. Bloomington, IN: Indiana University Press.

Ballard, Kim (2016). 'Rhetoric, power and persuasion in *Julius Caesar*'. *The British Library, Discovering Literature: Shakespeare & Renaissance* (15 March). Available at: https://www.bl.uk/shakespeare/articles/rhetoric-power-and-persuasion-in-julius-caesar.

Barrett Browning, Elizabeth (2011 [1890]). 'A Vision of Poets'. In *Elizabeth Barrett Browning's Poetical Works Vol. I* [ebook], Project Gutenberg edn. Available at: https://www.gutenberg.org/files/37452/37452-h/37452-h.htm.

Barthes, Roland (1977). 'The Death of the Author'. In *Image-Music-Text*, tr. Stephen Heath. London: Fontana, pp. 142–148.

Barton, John (2000). *Playing Shakespeare*. York: Methuen Drama.

BBC Teach (n.d.). 'Why is the Bard so popular abroad?'. Available at: https://www.bbc.co.uk/teach/why-is-the-bard-so-poular-abroad/zhcjrj6.

Bickley, Pamela and Stevens, Jenny (2020). *Studying Shakespeare in Adaptation: From Restoration Theatre to YouTube*. London: Bloomsbury.

Blackman, Malorie (2017). *Chasing the Stars*. London: Penguin.

Blackman, Malorie (2001). *Noughts & Crosses*. London: Penguin.

Bloom, Harold (2017). *Falstaff: Give Me Life*. New York: Scribner.

Bloom, Harold (2001). *Shakespeare: The Invention of the Human*. London: Penguin.

Bloom, Harold (1994). *The Western Canon: The Books and School of the Ages*. London: Harcourt, Brace & Co.

Bradbury, Ray (2015). *Something Wicked This Ways Comes*. London: Gollancz.

Brown, Mark (2016). 'Shakespeare more popular abroad than in Britain, study finds', *The Guardian* (19 April). Available at: https://www.theguardian.com/culture/2016/apr/19/shakespeare-popular-china-mexico-turkey-than-uk-british-council-survey#:~:text=The%20report%2C%20called%20All%20the,countries%20on%20an%20unprecedented%20scale.

Browning, Robert (1904). 'House'. In Bliss Carman (ed.), *The World's Best Poetry, Vol. VII: Descriptive Poems, Narrative Poems*. Philadelphia: John D. Morris & Co. Available at: https://www.bartleby.com/360/7/79.html.

Bruner, Jerome (1960). *The Process of Education*. New York: Vintage Books.

Bryson, Bill (2007). *Shakespeare: The World as Stage*. New York: Atlas Books.

Campbell, Joseph (2012). *The Hero with a Thousand Faces*, 3rd edn. Novato, CA: New World Library.

Carroll, Robert and Prickett, Stephen (eds.) (1997). *The Bible: Authorised King James Version*. Oxford: Oxford University Press.

Carter, Angela (1992). *Wise Children*. London: Penguin Vintage Classics.

Castelow, Ellen (n.d.). 'Shakespeare, Richard II and Rebellion'. *Historic UK*. Available at: https://www.historic-uk.com/HistoryUK/HistoryofEngland/Shakespeare-Richard-II-Rebellion/.

Chambers, Aidan (1995). *Book Talk: Occasional Writing on Literature and Children*. Woodchester: Thimble Press.

Chevalier, Tracey (2018). *New Boy*. London: Vintage Press.

Coe, Rob, Rauch, C. J., Kime, Stuart and Singleton, Dan (2020). *Great Teaching Toolkit: Evidence Review*. Available at: https://assets.website-files.com/5ee28729f7b4a5fa99bef2b3/5ee9f507021911ae35ac6c4d_EBE_GTT_EVIDENCE%20REVIEW_DIGITAL.pdf?utm_referrer=https%3A%2F%2Fwww.greatteaching.com.

Cummings, Brian (2016). 'The Reformation in Shakespeare', *British Library* (15 March). Available at: https://www.bl.uk/shakespeare/articles/the-reformation-in-shakespeare.

de Grazia, Margreta and Wells, Stanley (eds.) (2010). *The Cambridge Companion to Shakespeare*. Cambridge: Cambridge University Press.

Department for Education (2010). *Developing Drama in English: A Handbook for Subject Leaders and Teachers*. Available at: https://dera.ioe.ac.uk/779/7/431361fb6069ab0e0b57b230e8ab5aab_Redacted.pdf.

Department for Education (2019). *Early Career Framework*. Available at: https://assets.publishing.service.gov.uk/government/uploads/system/uploads/attachment_data/file/978358/Early-Career_Framework_April_2021.pdf.

Department for Education (2019). *ITT Core Content Framework*. Available at: https://assets.publishing.service.gov.uk/government/uploads/system/uploads/attachment_data/file/974307/ITT_core_content_framework_.pdf.

Dickinson, Emily (1998). 'Tell all the truth but tell it slant'. In *The Poems of Emily Dickinson: Reading Edition*, ed. Ralph W. Franklin. Cambridge, MA: The Belknap Press of Harvard University Press. Available at: https://www.poetryfoundation.org/poems/56824/tell-all-the-truth-but-tell-it-slant-1263.

Duffy, Carol Ann (1999). 'Anne Hathaway' in *The World's Wife*. New York: Macmillan, p. 24.

Eagleton, Terry (2008). *Literary Theory: An Introduction*, 2nd edn. New Jersey: Wiley-Blackwell.

Edmondson, Paul, Dr, and Chouhan, Anjna, Dr. (2020–2021). 'Conversations about Shakespeare's Place in the 21st Century' *Shakespeare Alive* [podcast]. Available at: https://www.shakespeare.org.uk/explore-shakespeare/podcasts/shakespeare-alive/?gclid=CjwKCAjw7rWKBhAtEiwAJ3CWLEiL-NUg353m3yJ52mm66AJAhtRMZf-kgw53LV3Lh4ZCxgoVyxDLchoCJQ8QAvD_BwE

Education Endowment Foundation (2017). *Metacognition and Self-Regulated Learning* (27 April). Available at https://educationendowmentfoundation.org.uk/education-evidence/guidance reports/metacognition.

Egan, Gabriel (2006). *Green Shakespeare: From Ecopolitics to Ecocriticism*. Abingdon and New York: Routledge.

Enser, Zoe and Enser, Mark (2020). *Fiorella & Mayer's Generative Learning in Action*. Woodbridge: John Catt Educational.

Fletcher, Anthony (1999). *Gender, Sex and Subordination: in England 1500–1800*. New Haven: Yale University Press.

Follows, Stephen (2014). 'How many movies based on Shakespeare's plays are there?', *Film Data and Education* (14 April). Available at: https://stephenfollows.com/movies-based-on-shakespeare-plays/#:~:text=Of%20the%20movies%20based%20on,film%20adaptations%20of%20Shakespeare%20plays.

Freud, Sigmund (1958). 'The Theme of the Three Caskets'. In *The Standard Edition of the Complete Psychological Works of Sigmund Freud, Volume XII (1922–1913)*. London: The Hogarth Press and The Institute of Pyscho-Analysis. Available at: https://www.sas.upenn.edu/~cavitch/pdf-library/Freud_ThreeCaskets.pdf.

Garfield, Leon (1997). *Shakespeare Stories*. London: Puffin Books.

Gillespie, Stuart (2003). *Shakespeare's Books: A Dictionary of Shakespeare's Sources*. London: Bloomsbury.

Giroux, Robert (2000). 'The Man Who Knew Shakespeare'. *New York Times* (February 13). Available at: https://archive.nytimes.com/www.nytimes.com/books/00/02/13/bookend/bookend.html?_r=1.

Goldstein, Gary B. (2004). 'Did Queen Elizabeth Use the Theatre for Social and Political Propaganda?', *The Oxfordian* VII: 161. Available at: https://shakespeareoxfordfellowship.org/wp-content/uploads/Oxfordian2004_Goldstein-Propaganda.pdf.

Grammaticus, Saxo (2006 [1905]). *The Danish History, Books I–IX* [ebook], Project Gutenberg edn. Available at: https://www.gutenberg.org/files/1150/1150-h/1150-h.htm.

Greenblatt, Stephen (2019). *Tyrant: Shakespeare on Politics*. New York: W. W. Norton & Company.

Grimm, Jacob and Wilhelm (2009). *The Complete Fairy Tales of the Brothers Grimm*. Hertfordshire: Wordsworth Classics.

Hadfield, Andrew (2003). *Shakespeare and Renaissance Politics*. London: Bloomsbury.

Healey, Margaret (2001). *Fictions of Disease in Early Modern England: Bodies, Plagues and Politics*. London: Palgrave.

Hogarth Shakespeare Series (launched 2015). Penguin Random House. Available at: https://www.penguinrandomhouse.com/series/HSR/hogarth-shakespeare.

Hopkins, Lisa and Hiscock, Andrew (eds.). *Arden Early Modern Drama Guides*. London: Bloomsbury.

Hughes, Haili (2022). *GCSE English Literature Boost*. Abingdon and New York: Routledge.

Huxley, Aldous (2007). *Brave New World* (London: Penguin Vintage Classics, 2007)

Into Film (n.d.). 'Shakespeare on screen'. Available at: https://www.intofilm.org/films/filmlist/11?gclid=CjwKCAjw7rWKBhAtEiwAJ3CWLEOJcR4pB1LYpdmEaZ-QMyAC6sMJABGt-EZ54iA3efkeINDyR3l5uRoCSiMQAvD_BwE.

Jacobson, Howard (2016). *Shylock Is My Name*. London: Penguin Random House.

Jellerson, Donald (2011). 'Haunted History and the Birth of the Republic in Middleton's *Ghost of Lucrece*'. *Criticism* 53(1) (Winter): 53–82. Available at: https://www.jstor.org/stable/23131555?seq=1#metadata_info_tab_contents.

Jonson, Ben (2014 [1892]). 'De Shakespeare Nostrat'. In H. Morley (ed.), *Discoveries Made upon Men and Matter and Some Poems* [ebook], Project Gutenberg edn. Available at: https://www.gutenberg.org/files/5134/5134-h/5134-h.htm.

King Jr, Martin Luther (1991). *I Have a Dream*. New York: Harper One.

King, John N. (1984). 'Renewing Literary History' (a review of *The Power of Forms in the English Renaissance*, ed. Stephen Greenblatt). *Shakespeare Quarterly* 35(2): 237–239 at 237. Available at: https://doi.org/10.2307/2869941.

Kirschner, Paul, Sweller, John and Clark, Richard E. (2006). 'Why Minimal Instruction Doesn't Work'. *Educational Psychologist* 41(2): 75–86. Available at: http://dx.doi.org/10.1207/s15326985ep4102_1.

Lynch, Matthew (2020). 'The Motif of Birds in Macbeth'. *Litdrive* (7 November). Available at: https://litdrive.org.uk/remotecpd#.

McCrum, Robert (2016). 'Ten ways in which Shakespeare Changed the World'. *The Guardian* (17 April). Available at: https://www.theguardian.com/culture/2016/apr/17/ten-ways-shakespeare-changed-the-world.

MacGregor, Neil (2013). *Shakespeare's Restless World: A Portrait of an Era in Twenty Objects.* London: Viking.

Manga Shakespeare Series. London: SelfMadeHero Books.

Matthews, Andrew and Ross, Tony (2003). *The Shakespeare Stories.* New York: Orchard Books.

Milton, John (2003). *Paradise Lost.* London: Penguin Classics.

New Casebooks Series. Basingstoke: Macmillan. Available at: https://www.macmillanexplorers.com/new-casebooks/15375472.

Munro, John (ed.) (2007 [1909]). *The Shakespere Allusion Book: A Collection of Allusions to Shakespere from 1591–1700*, originally compiled by Clement Mansfield Ingleby, Lucy Toulmin Smith and Frederick J. Furnivall. London: Chatto & Windus.

National Geographic (n.d.). 'The Life and Reign of Queen Elizabeth I'. Available at: https://www.natgeokids.com/uk/discover/history/monarchy/elizabeth-i-facts/.

No Sweat Shakespeare (n.d.). 'Shakespeare's Use of Mythology'. *No Sweat Shakespeare* [blog]. Available at: https://nosweatshakespeare.com/blog/shakespeare-us-of-mythology/.

Ofsted (2021). *Education Inspection Framework* (updated 19 April). Available at: https://www.gov.uk/government/publications/education-inspection-framework/education-inspection-framework.

Ofsted (2021). *Research Review Series: History* (14 July). Available at: https://www.gov.uk/government/publications/research-review-series-history/research-review-series-history.

O'Reilly, Sally (2014). 'Top Ten Novels Inspired by Shakespeare', *The Guardian* (30 April). Available at: https://www.theguardian.com/books/2014/apr/30/top-10-novels-inspired-shakespeare-herman-melville-patricia-highsmith.

Ortiz, Joseph M. (2016). *Shakespeare and the Culture of Romanticism.* Abingdon: Routledge.

Packer, Tina (2016). *Women of Will: The Remarkable Evolution of Shakespeare's Female Characters.* New York: Vintage Books.

Pinker, Steven (2015). *The Sense of Style: The Thinking Person's Guide to Writing in the 21st Century.* London: Penguin.

Pinkett, Matt and Roberts, Mark (2019). *Boys Don't Try? Rethinking Masculinity in Schools.* Abingdon: Routledge.

Porter, Roy (2003). *Madness: A Brief History.* Oxford: Oxford University Press.

Pressley, J. M. (n.d.). 'Biblical Shakespeare', *Shakespeare Resource Centre.* Available at: https://www.bardweb.net/content/ac/shakesbible.html.

Propp, Vladimir (1968). *Morphology of the Folk Tale*, tr. Laurence Scott. Bloomington, IN: The American Folklore Society and Indiana University.

Pryke, Stuart and Staniforth, Amy (2020). *Ready to Teach: Macbeth: A Compendium of Subject Knowledge, Resources and Pedagogy*. Woodbridge: John Catt Educational.

Rai, Bali (2004). *Rani and Sukh*. London: Corgi.

Reynolds, Jason (2018). *Long Way Down*. London: Faber & Faber.

Rhys, Jean (2000). *Wide Sargasso Sea*. London: Penguin Classics.

Rickert, Edith (1923). 'Political Propaganda and Satire in *A Midsummer Night's Dream* II'. *Modern Philology* 21(2): 133–154.

Rogers, Jamie (2022). *British Black and Asian Shakespeareans: 1966–2018*. London: Bloomsbury.

Rose, Mary Beth (1991). 'Where are the Mothers in Shakespeare? Options for Gender Representation in the English Renaissance'. *Shakespeare Quarterly* 42(3): 291–314

Rosenshine, Barak (2012). 'Principles of Instruction: Research-Based Strategies That All Teachers Should Know'. *American Educator* 36: 12–39.

Royal Museums Greenwich. 'Queen Elizabeth I's speech to the troops at Tilbury'. Available at: https://www.rmg.co.uk/stories/topics/queen-elizabeth-speech-troops-tilbury.

Schwarz, Michael (2020). 'A plague on both your houses'. *Guided by Art* [blog] (1 May). Available at: https://beguidedbyart.com/a-plague-on-both-your-houses/.

Senechal, Heloise (2008). 'Biblical and Classical References'. *The Royal Shakespeare Company*. Taken from *The Complete Works of Shakespeare*. RSC, Macmillan. Available at: https://www.rsc.org.uk/shakespeare/language/biblical-and-classical-references.

Shakespeare's Globe. Virtual Tour. Available at: https://www.shakespearesglobe.com/discover/about-us/virtual-tour/.

Shakespeare Study Guide. 'Shakespeare Essays and Commentary Online'. Available at: http://shakespearestudyguide.com/Shake2/Shakespeare%20Essays%20Online.html.

Shakespeare, William (1992). *The Complete Works of Shakespeare*. London: Magpie Books.

Shakespeare, William (1916). In W. J. Craig (ed. with a glossary), *The Complete Works of William Shakespeare (The Oxford Shakespeare)*. Oxford: Oxford University Press. Available at: https://oll4.libertyfund.org/title/craig-the-complete-works-of-william-shakespeare-the-oxford-shakespeare.

Shakespeare, William (1623). *Mr. William Shakespeares Comedies, Histories, & Tragedies. Published According to the True Originall Copies* [The First Folio]. London: Issac and William Jaggard and Edward Blount.

Shapiro, James (2015). *The Year of Lear: Shakespeare in 1606*. London: Simon & Schuster.

Smith, Bruce R. (2000). *Shakespeare and Masculinity*. Oxford: Oxford University Press.

Smith, Emma (2010–2017). *Approaching Shakespeare* [podcast]. University of Oxford. Available at: https://podcasts.ox.ac.uk/series/approaching-shakespeare.

Smith, Emma (2020). *This is Shakespeare: How to Read the World's Greatest Playwright*. New Orleans: Pelican Books.

Snyder, Susan (1979). *The Comic Matrix of Shakespeare's Tragedies: Romeo and Juliet, Hamlet, Othello, and King Lear*. Princeton, NJ: Princeton University Press.

SparkNotes (2004). *No Fear Shakespeare: Much Ado About Nothing*. New York: SparkNotes. Also available online at: https://www.sparknotes.com/nofear/shakespeare/muchado/.

Stoppard, Tom (1973). *Rosencrantz and Guildenstern are Dead.* London: Faber & Faber.

Struever, Nancy S. (1988). 'Shakespeare and Rhetoric'. *Rhetorica: A Journal of the History of Rhetoric* 6(2): 137–144. Available at: https://www.jstor.org/stable/10.1525/rh.1988.6.issue-2.

Symonds, Arthur (2007). *The Poems of Samuel Taylor Coleridge.* Charleston, SC: BiblioBazaar.

Teacher Development Trust (2014). *Developing Great Teaching: Lessons from the International Reviews into Effective Professional Development.* Available at: https://tdtrust.org/wp-content/uploads/2015/10/DGT-Summary.pdf.

Tennenhouse, Leonard (1985). 'Strategies of State and Political Plays'. In Jonathan Dollimore and Alan Sinfield (eds.), *Political Shakespeare: New Essays in Cultural Materialism.* Manchester: Manchester University Press, pp. 109–128.

Terry, Ellen (1932). 'The Triumphant Women'. In Christopher St John (ed.), *Four Lectures on Shakespeare.* London: Martin Hopkinson, p. 81.

Todorov, Tzvetan (1975). *The Fantastic: A Structural Approach to a Literary Genre,* tr. Richard Howard. New York: Cornell University Press.

Webb, Jennifer (2019). *How to Teach English Literature: Overcoming Cultural Poverty.* Woodbridge: John Catt Educational.

Willis, Matthew (2020). 'Making Sense of the Divine Right of Kings'. *JSTOR Daily* (18 December). Available at: https://daily.jstor.org/making-sense-of-the-divine-right-of-kings/.

Winters, Cat (2016). *The Steep and Thorny Way.* New York: Amulet Books.

Wordsworth, William (1827). 'Scorn not the Sonnet'. Available at: https://rpo.library.utoronto.ca/content/scorn-not-sonnet.

Young, Michael and Lambert, David (2014). *Knowledge and the Future School: Curriculum and Social Justice.* London: Bloomsbury.

Additional Resources

Akala (2011). 'Hip-Hop and Shakespeare', *TEDx Aldeburgh Talk* [video] (7 December). Available at: https://www.youtube.com/watch?v=DSbtkLA3GrY.

BBC Sounds. The Shakespeare Sessions (free dramatisations and discussions of the plays for account holders). Available at: https://www.bbc.co.uk/sounds/brand/p0655br3.

British Council. Shakespeare Key Stage 2 materials. Available at: https://learnenglishkids.britishcouncil.org/category/topics/shakespeare.

British Library. 'Brooke's Romeus and Juliet'. Available at: https://www.bl.uk/collection-items/brookes-romeus-and-juliet.

British Library. 'Hollinshed's Chronicles, 1577'. Available at: https://www.bl.uk/collection-items/holinsheds-chronicles-1577.

British Library. 'Ovid's Metamorphoses'. Available at: https://www.bl.uk/collection-items/ovids-metamorphoses.

British Library. 'Printed edition of King James VI and I's Basilikon Doron or 'The King's Gift', 1603. Available at: https://www.bl.uk/collection-items/printed-edition-of-king-james-vi-and-is-basilikon-doron-or-the-kings-gift-1603.

British Library. 'Shakespeare's Life and World'. Available at: https://www.bl.uk/shakespeare/themes/context.

British Library. 'The Geneva Bible, 1570'. Available at: https://www.bl.uk/collection-items/the-geneva-bible-1570#:~:text=There%20are%20many%20Biblical%20references,often%20closest%20to%20this%20text.

Duncan, Sophie (2020). Comedy in Shakespeare's Twelfth Night, *Massolit* [video] (7 October). Available at: https://www.youtube.com/watch?v=vkvPvuDj6Nc.

Editors of Encyclopaedia Britannica, 'Shakespeare's plays and poems of William Shakespeare', *Encyclopedia Britannica*. Available at: https://www.britannica.com/biography/William-Shakespeare/Shakespeares-plays-and-poems.

Edmondson, Paul and Chouhan, Anina (2020–2021). 'Conversations about Shakespeare's Place in the 21st Century', *Shakespeare Alive* [podcast]. Available at: https://www.shakespeare.org.uk/explore-shakespeare/podcasts/shakespeare-alive/?gclid=CjwKCAjw7rWKBhAtEiwAJ3CWLEiL-NUg353m3yJ52mm66AJAhtRMZf-kgw53LV3Lh4ZCxgoVyxDLchoCJQ8QAvD_BwE.

National Theatre. National Theatre Collection. Available at: https://www.nationaltheatre.org.uk/learning/national-theatre-collection.

Shakespeare: The Animated Tales (BBC, 1992–1994).

Shakespeare Essays and Commentary Online. The Shakespeare Study Guide. Available at: http://shakespearestudyguide.com/Shake2/Shakespeare%20Essays%20Online.html.

Shakespeare: The Animated Tales (1992–1994) [TV series]. BBC.

Storytelling Schools. Available at: https://storytellingschools.com/.

TES Teaching Resources. Available at: https://www.tes.com/teaching-resource/literary-criticism-a-level-feminism-marxism-psychoanalysis-queer-theory-etc-11581782.

The Life and Times of William Shakespeare (2015). Dir. Liam Dale [documentary]. Available at: https://www.youtube.com/watch?v=vKBU5SirBFo.

Index of Entries